MALCOLM BOYD wrote the prayers in ARE YOU RUNNING WITH ME, JESUS? out of his commitment to both God and contemporary concerns. The book became a much discussed bestseller, and seems certain to become a classic of modern religious expression. Robert McAfee Brown said, "This book destroys the conventional distance between prayer and 'ordinary life.'... There are few books of prayers I would give to a friend. This is one of them." In this spirit of ecumenicism *Ave Maria's* review said, "These are contemporary prayers that touch the heart of modern man and express his feelings to God in a direct, meaningful experience." The *Detroit News* said, "Run out today and buy this book... and buy another copy as a gift for your minister, your rabbi, or your priest."

There is something in ARE YOU RUNNING WITH ME, JESUS? that has made these prayers an integral part of many different lives. It is perhaps Malcolm Boyd himself, for the prayers are mirrors of his devotion, his enthusiasm, and his love for God and modern man.

ARE YOU RUNNING WITH ME, JESUS?

Prayers by Malcolm Boyd

An Avon Library Book

AVON BOOKS
A division of
The Hearst Corporation
959 Eighth Avenue
New York, New York 10019

First Avon Library Edition, February, 1967

Cover photo by Robert L. Frank

Printed in Canada.

To the Freedom Struggle—

the persons who have been close to me in the struggle including John, Henri, Kim, Paul and Jenny, Jonathan, Claude, Woodie, Reg, Arthur, Bill, Quinland, Layton, Naomi and Richard

the institutions embodying the struggle and particularly the Student Non-Violent Coordinating Committee, Students for a Democratic Society, the Delta Ministry of the National Council of Churches, the Commission on Religion and Race of the National Council of Churches, and the Episcopal Society for Cultural and Racial Unity

■ Contents

ARE YOU RUNNING WITH ME, JESUS?

◼ Introduction

I cannot recall exactly when the idea, and way, of prayer began to change radically in my own life.

Prayer, for me, used to stand as something separate from other parts of life. But I have come to learn that real prayer is not so much talking to God as just sharing his presence. More and more, prayer and my style of life as a Christian now seem inseparable.

This assertion may seem to smack of self-righteousness, as if I have it "made." I don't mean it that way. It is simply an awareness that Christ *has* it "made," and my life is a life *in his*, not at all by any goodness or merits on my part but because of his love. Thus I am able to live in a kind of Christian nonchalance rooted in a trust of God which severs the old double-standard morality game I used to play with him. I can no longer conceive of lying to him in proper Old English or any other style of speech. I feel free to be completely myself with him. In a given situation where I know he is with me (perhaps in another person, or persons), I speak out of that deep trust and love which can spring only from a healthy, tried, and authentic freedom.

During a Freedom Ride in the Deep South in 1961, one of my fellow Episcopalian priests said: "It seems to me this is really a kind of prayer—a kind of corporate confession of sin." Some people said the Freedom

Ride was essentially a sermon. But my fellow priest well expressed my feelings about being on that bus. It was a prayer.

In 1964, I attended a Roman Catholic Mass in Lebanon. During the liturgy, someone gave me the "kiss of peace," which I was to pass along to the next person. As the man on my right embraced me, he said the traditional words: "The Lord be with you." I replied with traditional correctness: "And with thy spirit." Then, turning to the man on my left, I said: "The Lord be with you." He replied—and I shall never forget the devastating honesty and directness of it: "And with you too, Malcolm." He was a layman, just then undertaking voluntary poverty, a member of a Roman Catholic group of priests and laymen with whom I was visiting Israel, the Near East, and Rome. The trip was an ecumenical encounter and discovery of singular grace. Something else had occurred to disturb and shake my prayer life.

In recent years I have had to spend much time traveling on planes from city to city, with the inevitable waiting in crowded but impersonal and lonely airports, and nights spent in innumerable faceless hotels. I came to realize that, for me, "community" was no longer an ideal but a reality, *here, now*. Each evening when I talked with groups of students, this was it—the sharing, the common life experienced together. I no longer had to seek for it; it was *given* and I had only to accept it. This molded my developing idea of prayer, too. Prayer could no longer be offered to God *up there* but to God *here*; prayer had to be natural and real, not phony or contrived; it was not about *other things* (as a rationalized fantasy or escape) but *these* things, however unattractive, jarring, or even socially outcast they might be.

God, I discovered, was not an upper-middle-class snob in a private, clublike "holy of holies" nor was he an impersonal I.B.M. machine computing petty sins in some celestial office building above the clouds. It came home to me that God was loving, in a terribly unsentimental and profound way. Every day, then, was like Good Friday's cross in demonstrating the depth and complexity and holy simplicity of his love.

I came to realize that many prayers are uttered without the prescribed forms of piety and even in a language which Puritans might, in their rigidity and lovelessness, label as profane. For example, Jerry's monologue in Edward Albee's play, *The Zoo Story*, is a prayer. If you will listen, you can hear prayers in the novels, songs, plays, and films of Samuel Beckett, Ralph Ellison, Ingmar Bergman, Saul Bellow, Bob Dylan, Tennessee Williams, James Baldwin, William Golding, Michelangelo Antonioni, Jean Genet, or John Updike. Prayer bridges the heretical gulf between the sacred and secular, the holy and profane. Of course, to hear some prayers, verbal or nonverbal, you must *listen* for what was not said.

Naïve and superstitious misconceptions about prayer have never ceased to shock me. On one occasion a forty-year-old man, an intellectual and cultural leader, confessed that he had stood in agony at his young son's grave, unable to pray because he did not know the words of a single prayer.

I am angered, as are many students and other youths, by worshipers who deny in their actions outside church what they "pray" about for one hour a week inside expensive Gothic or Colonial buildings. There is a hypocritical gulf between mouthing verbal prayers about Negroes and then resolutely manipulating a white power structure to keep Negroes in housing ghettos and interminable second-class citizenship.

During my stay at the Taizé Community in France, in 1957, I learned how the integrity of grace before meal was linked to an action of fasting. Prayer was offered on the fast day for persons in Asia who were literally starving to death. This grace, coupled with fasting from lunch, expressed solidarity with them in prayer.

Some devout Christians believe that prayer is practicing the presence of God, and they find it difficult to enter into circumscribed or particular forms of prayer which seem to say, "Prayer is commencing now." Haven't they been involved in prayer all the time? On the other hand, one Christian clergyman saw things quite differently. "My prayers are addressed either to a Lord whom I do not perceive at all," he told me, "and I speak them into the void with a blind and sometimes desperate faith, or else, in my more mystical moments, with a sense of awe and wonder to Jesus Christ."

Prayer, I have learned, is more my response to God than a matter of my own initiative. I believe Jesus Christ prays *in* me as well as *for* me. But my response is sporadic, moody, now despairing, now joyful, corrupted by my self-love and desire to manipulate Christ's love. The community of Christ incarnates prayer in its essential life, and my own prayer is a part of this. But many times when I am caught up in egoism and self-pity, I forget. I find in the Psalms much the same range of mood and expression as I perceive within my own life of prayer.

14 ■

God's grace is wonderful in prayer as in all other parts of human life. I remember a Sunday morning in 1964, during a trip to Mississippi to assist in Negro voter registration. At the "Freedom House" where I lived, I became deeply involved in a conversation with one of the student volunteers. She had not talked with an older person for quite some time about the things that mattered most to her, the pressing personal questions about life. She had so much to say that by the time we finished it was too late for me to attend morning worship.

It had remained in my mind that it was Sunday morning, and I had planned to attend a worship service, although I knew it must be a Negro service *or* a white one. As always, I hated this particular sinful prospect. But then, suddenly, God's grace seemed simply and beautifully manifest to me. The student and I had broken toast and eaten it, had shared the coffee. Surely God had, in his providence and merciful love, permitted us to share in communion with him.

It has been asked by some persons why this book is not entitled *Am I Running With You, Jesus?* The query overlooks the fact that my prayer life, as the state of my spirituality, is neither very respectable nor quite correct. Needless to say, I am a self-centered man, sinfully immersed in my own welfare and concerns, attempting to manipulate God, and often lost in my own self-love and self-pity. *Are You Running With Me, Jesus?* more accurately reflects the grounding, motivation, and style of my prayer life and spirituality as I grapple with imperfections and ambiguities in myself and my society.

The prayers which follow are some of my experiences

in prayer. They are not meant for anyone else to recite by rote or copy as from a blueprint; these can only be signposts, pointing toward those elements I find in church renewal and in church tradition, which can somehow be brought into a unity of worship.

Each of us is a person, with individual masks, scars, celebrations, moments of rejecting God, and experiences of conversion. Our prayers must spring from the indigenous soil of our own personal confrontation with the Spirit of God in our lives. Even for myself the words printed here are not wholly and completely those prayers. They are approximations or recollections of these, adaptations of some, and paraphrases of others. They stand for something deeper which can never be captured in writing or even fully in the spontaneously spoken word.

I have not attempted to root out the person of Malcolm Boyd from these prayers, for it was Malcolm Boyd who prayed them. Prayer must be personal, imbedded in the ground of one's own being as a person meeting God. These prayers are not intended as impersonal exhibits in a vacuum. They are the prayers of one man. It is hoped they may be useful, as signposts, to other men and women.

Prayers for the Free Self

It's morning, Jesus. It's morning, and here's that light and sound all over again

■ I've got to move fast . . . get into the bathroom, wash up, grab a bite to eat, and run some more.

■ I just don't feel like it, Lord. What I really want to do is to get back into bed, pull up the covers, and sleep. All I seem to want today is the big sleep, and here I've got to run all over again.

■ Where am I running? You know these things I can't understand. It's not that I need to have you tell me. What counts most is just that somebody knows, and it's you. That helps a lot.

■ So I'll follow along, okay? But lead, Lord. Now I've got to run. Are you running with me, Jesus?

I'm crying and shouting inside tonight, Lord, and I'm feeling completely alone

■ All the roots I thought I had are gone. Everything in my life is in an upheaval. I am amazed that I can maintain any composure when I'm feeling like this.

■ The moment is all that matters; the present moment is of supreme importance. I know this. Yet in the present I feel dead. I want to anchor myself in the past and shed tears of self-pity. When I look ahead tonight I can see only futility, pain, and death. I am only a rotting body, a vessel of disease, potentially a handful of ashes after I am burned.

■ But you call me tonight to love and responsibility. You have a job for me to do. You make me look at other persons whose needs make my self-pity a mockery and a disgrace.

■ Lord, I hear you. I know you. I feel your presence strongly in this awful moment, and I thank you. Help me onto my feet. Help me to get up.

You said there is perfect freedom in your service, Lord

■ Well, I don't feel perfectly free. I don't feel free at all. I'm a captive to myself.

■ I do what I want. I have it all my own way. There is no freedom at all for me in this, Jesus. Today I feel like a slave bound in chains and branded by a hot iron because I'm a captive to my own will and don't give an honest damn about you or your will.

■ You're over there where I'm keeping you, outside my real life. How can I go on being such a lousy hypocrite? Come over here, where I don't want you to come. Let me quit playing this blasphemous game of religion with you. Jesus, help me to let you be yourself in my life—so that I can be myself.

I know it sounds corny, Jesus, but I'm lonely

■ I wasn't going to get lonely any more, and so I kept very busy, telling myself I was serving you. But it's getting dark again, and I'm alone; honestly, Lord, I'm lonely as hell.

■ Why do I feel so sorry for myself? There's no reason why I should be. You're with me, and I know it. I'll be with other people in a little while. I know some of them love me very much in their own way, and I love some of them very much in mine.

■ But I still feel so damned lonely right now, in this minute that I'm living. I feel confused about how to get through the immediate next few steps to the other ones afterward. It's silly, but I feel this way because I'm threatened by me, and I wish I could get through me to you, clearly and with a kind of purity and integrity.

■ And yet, while I say this to you, I've been unkind to certain people whom you also love, and I've added to misunderstanding and confusion, and I haven't been able to make it at all nicely or properly.

■ Take hold of me, and connect me with these other lives, Jesus. Give me patience and love so that I can listen when I plug into these other lives. Help me to listen and listen and listen . . . and love by being quiet and serving, and being there.

I'm scared, Jesus. You've asked me to do something I don't think I can do

■ I'm sure I wouldn't want to do it except that you asked me.

■ But I don't feel strong enough, and you know that I lack the courage I'd need. Why did you ask me to do this? It seems to me that John could do this much, much more easily, Lord. Remember, I told you I'm afraid to stand up and be criticized, Jesus. I feel naked in front of everybody, and I can't hide any part of myself.

■ Why can't I be quiet and have peace and be left alone? I don't see what good it will do for me to be dragged out in front of everybody and do this for you. Don't misunderstand me. I'm not saying I won't do it. I'm just saying I don't *want* to do it. I mean, how in hell *can* I do it?

■ You know me better than anybody does, but then you go and ask me to do something crazy like this. I can't figure you out. I wish you'd just leave me alone today, but if this is what you think is best, I'll try. I'll try. But I don't want to. Pray for me, Jesus.

The drinks are tranquilizing me, Lord, relaxing me and helping me to take it

■ But even while I'm being tranquilized, I don't want to be.

■ I remember the cutting edge you lived on. You didn't get tranquilized. You went right on taking it, and then you gave back love. I seem to have run out of love, and I'm certainly taking it very badly right now.

■ Don't leave me alone, Christ, because I've left you. I just want the easy way out, any way out at all, but you know I really don't. I hurt inside and wish I could tear myself away.

■ This isn't me here, Jesus. This really isn't me. You know it, but nobody else does. I'm putting on a good act, but you know what a lousy act it really is.

■ Get me back to my own cutting edge, Lord. Help me to put away the tranquilizers and just be myself with you and the others you place me with.

I'm having a ball, and I just want to thank you, Jesus

■ This is a good day for me. Yesterday I was down, but today I'm up again. These people I'm with are the greatest. The sun has really come out for me. I see everything in bright reds and yellows.

■ I hated the dark reds and the crying blues yesterday. I was mean, Lord, and vicious, and I can hardly understand how anybody put up with me. But they didn't beat me down. They let me know what it is to be human because *they* stayed human. Now I'm human again. I feel good, and I want to get out with the people and swing with them, Jesus.

■ There's somebody I was mean to yesterday. I want to knock myself out to be nice to him today. Honestly, Lord, thank you.

I want to be alone and not to be alone, both at the same time

■ I can't stand anybody being around at this moment. The sound of another voice seems to cut into my aching flesh. I want to be alone. I crave silence, even a vacuum, an endless echo chamber of silence upon silence upon silence. Cold. Alone. Silence.

■ But this silence is filled with demons, Lord, so that I'm not alone at all. I'm with demons. And I'd rather be with other people, Jesus, and with you. I've thought it out, and this is what I want. Will you help me cut loose from these demons so I can be with you and the other people?

■ I feel so cold, and I want to warm myself by a fire, Lord. Please give me the fire to thaw out the icy coldness inside me. Warm me, Jesus, so I can give out some real warmth to some other very cold people.

The blood ran to my head, Lord, and I almost flipped

■ I was mad and couldn't think clearly. Thanks for cooling me down.

■ If I'd been on my own, I would have done something bad to somebody whom you love just as much as me. I was very vulnerable, Jesus, and he didn't realize he'd hit me in a spot so soft I should put up a neon sign over it that flashes "danger" twenty-four hours a day.

■ He hit, and I screamed inside, which is the worst kind of screaming. Then the heat flashed, and I couldn't make sense and just wanted revenge. I wanted to hurt him, Jesus.

■ When I simmered down, I was still sitting there, and he was still sitting there. I knew I was okay, that I hadn't done anything that would really louse everybody up.

■ Thank you, Lord, for being there with me and cooling me down. Thanks for taking hold of me.

I'm nowhere, Lord, and I couldn't care less

■ It's so still. Am I on the moon? Am I on the earth? Am I *here* at all? But, if so, where?

■ I feel disengaged from life at this moment, Lord. Time has stopped, and nothing matters. I have nowhere to hurry, no place to go, no sensible goal. I might as well be dead.

■ I want to feel a breeze blow against my face, or the hot sun warming me. I want to feel life, Jesus. Help me to feel love or anger or laughter. Help me to care about life again.

I'm exhausted, Jesus, but sleep won't come

■ My brain keeps whirring with thoughts, and it won't turn off. I have to get up early in the morning, and I'm desperate for a good night's rest. I can't get cool. I keep telling myself to quiet down and drop off, but it just won't work.

■ I keep rotating, Jesus, first on my stomach, then on my back, then on my side, and on my other side, and on my stomach again. I can't lie still.

■ The night is going to slip away, and pretty soon the light will come, and I'll be dead tired, Lord. I'm worried, and I can't let go. So many things on my mind. What's going to happen, Jesus? What's going to happen? No, you're right, I'm not looking for an answer. Help me to stop asking. Turn me off.

■ Lord, bless my sleep. Let me sleep. Help me to sleep. And then wake me up when the light comes, will you? Please wake me up, and let me be refreshed in your strength.

It's bumper to bumper, and the traffic is stalled

■ My radio is on and, yes, I'm listening to the news again. In a few minutes there'll be some more music.

■ I want to get home, Lord, but the traffic won't move. I'm tired from working, tired of waiting, tired of listening to the stupid radio. I'm too damned tired to be patient, and I'm hot and sweaty. I've worked hard all day, and I want to get home. I don't feel like being loving or patient or kind or long-suffering. Not right now. Later, maybe.

■ If I could have anything in the world right now, it would be a road stretching out ahead, empty, all other cars gone, and a beautiful freeway for miles and miles, just for me, and then *home*. I've just about had it today. Really, it's too much. Don't ask me to be patient.

■ Okay, I'll try some more to be human, but it's nearly been knocked out of me for one day. Stay with me; I can't do it alone.

■ Jesus, thanks for sweating it out with me out here on this highway.

This record sends me, Jesus, but the magic doesn't last

■ It gives me the big build-up, and then it really tears me down to the foundations all the way.

■ Why does it send me this way? What is it saying and doing to me? All right, I know I'm using it for the build-up, but isn't that understandable? I need the build-up now, and it's only a record—it's only music, so what's wrong with using it?

■ Can't I have an escape?

■ Lord, don't leave me alone while I'm trying to kid myself. Please stay with me while I play my games. Please be with me in my games, because they hurt me and I have to face myself when they're over. And, frankly, Lord, that's when I'm scared the most.

I'm grateful things broke this way, Lord

■ I didn't know quite what to do before. Nothing would give at all. Nothing would give an inch. Everything was stymied and, Jesus, I was, too.

■ Everything had been gray for so long. Nothing was going my way at all, and I felt so permanently lousy.

■ Thanks, Jesus, for the sun coming out. Thanks for this real break and for making me feel alive again.

Jesus, it's evening again

■ What happened to this day? I'm not sure I found you in it, as it was moving and I was moving, too. I'm not at all clear whether I loved my fellow man today or got involved in life in the way I know you wanted me to do. Maybe I just kept life moving along. But, if so, *why?*

■ Now I'm too tired to think about it rationally. Tomorrow is coming close: Will it be the same? But, if so, *why?*

■ I become frightened, Jesus, as the day ends and I feel my life being spent, and my human time draining away. I feel so small in an age of science and space, and sometimes wonder what possible meaning I can have. Help me to understand what it means for you to be the lord of science and space, and the whole of life. And of this evening, even with its fears.

■ **Prayers for the Free Society**

What was Hiroshima like, Jesus, when the bomb fell?

■ What went through the minds of mothers, what happened to the lives of children, what stabbed at the hearts of men when they were caught up in a sea of flames?

■ What was Auschwitz like, Jesus, when the crematoriums belched the stinking smoke from the burned bodies of people? When families were separated, the weak perished, the strong faced inhuman tortures of the spirit and the body. What was the concentration camp like, Jesus?

■ Tell us, Lord, that we, the living, are capable of the same cruelty, the same horror, if we turn our back on you, our brother, and our other brothers. Save us from ourselves; spare us the evils of our hearts' good intentions, unbridled and mad. Turn us from our perversions of love, especially when these are perpetrated in your name. Speak to us about war, and about peace, and about the possibilities for both in our very human hearts.

Lord, we know you love the world that you created and redeemed

■ We who stand in the world offer ourselves and our society for your blessing and healing.

■ We confess that we have failed to love as you did. We have been socially unjust, and our society is imperfect, fragmented, and sometimes sick to death.

■ Teach us your ways in the world and in this life which we share together. Don't let us restrict you to a narrow ghetto labeled "religion," but lead us to worship you in the fullness of life as the lord of politics, economics, and the arts.

■ Give us light to seek true morality, not in narrow legalisms but in sacrifice and open responsibility. Show us how to express our love for you in very specific, human service to other men.

■ Lord, change our hearts from hearts of stone to hearts of flesh, and let us give thanks to you for all of life.

Work for him means hell, Lord

■ He's well paid. He never works up a sweat. His task is a relatively simple one—in fact, he doesn't see the connection between it and anyone else's task and any kind of a completed product. Between his work and the end result—a new car—there seems to be nothingness, a big void, an assembly line to oblivion.

■ Some joker at a union meeting one night said something corny about discovering the "Christian meaning" of work. He'd like to put that Christian talker on the assembly line for exactly three months, day by day, hour after hour. What would the guy have to say *then* about "Christian meaning"?

■ His work is monotony to the point that he sometimes thinks he'll fall asleep—that, or start running wild down the assembly line. His work on the line affects his whole life, Jesus. All of it seems to be a mean, devilish assembly line—getting up, driving to work, eight hours on the job, rest breaks and lunch, driving back home, looking at television, eating and sleeping. A fiery hell would be an exciting prospect for him to look forward to, Lord.

■ Can he be brought to life, Jesus? What could life and his work really mean to him?

She doesn't feel like an animal, Jesus, even though she's being treated like one

■ She looks sixty but she isn't yet forty years old. She is a migrant farm worker. She's working in this field all day—and day here means sunrise to sunset. Afterward, she'll go back with her family to spend the night in a one-room tin shack most people wouldn't let their dog live in.

■ Nothing seems to be gained by her suffering and deprivation, Jesus. She never gets ahead financially. The small amount of money taken in is already owed for back groceries. She needs a lot of medical care she'll never receive. Her husband is just as much a beast of burden as she. Their children seem already to be caught in the same vicious circle of exploitation.

■ There is still a vision of humanness inside her mind and soul, Jesus, although her body is broken and her face is wasted. Should she nourish any glimmer of hope, Lord, or would it be better for her to erase hope from her consciousness? What happens to a society which takes such a toll in human life and doesn't care?

Somebody forgot to push the right button, Jesus

■ So all hell broke loose. Airline schedules are loused up, somebody is shouting at somebody else who can't help the situation, a lot of money has been lost, and about two dozen people are caught up in a cybernetic tangle. We've missed our plane, which isn't our fault, and I was due in Chicago to participate in a meeting forty-five minutes ago.

■ Please cool everybody off, Lord, including me, since I'm one of the people involved, and I'm hot right now and shouting angrily at someone else who can't help the cybernetic crisis any more than I can.

■ And, Lord, please keep us human and capable of weathering such minor—and major—disasters. Don't let us turn ourselves into machines, no matter how hard we seem to be trying.

I'm with you in a television studio, Jesus

■ A star is out there in front right now, and the audience is responding with laughter. I'm a guest, nervously waiting to go on. Cameramen, prop men, men on lights, script girls, the director and his assistants, a publicity woman—they're all hard at work. Ad men are checking copies of commercials, and sponsors are watching in distant offices and homes.

■ Do all these people know you're here too, Lord? Would they willingly and knowingly present you with this show, along with their motives for working on it?

■ Thanks for being with all of us here in the studio, Jesus.

I've searched for community in many places, Jesus

■ I was often looking in the wrong places, but I don't think my motive was altogether wrong. I was looking futilely and hopelessly there for fellowship, belonging, and acceptance.

■ Now, in this moment, which many people would label "loneliness," or "nothingness," I want to thank you, Jesus. In this moment—in this place and with these other persons—I have found community where and as it is. It seems to me it is your gift.

■ I am here with these others for only a few hours. I will be gone tomorrow. But I won't be searching so desperately any more. I know I must accept community where you offer it to me. I accept it in this moment. Thank you, Jesus.

We can't make it alone, Lord

■ God knows, we've tried, and we've even reached the point where we could blow up everybody, including ourselves. Teach us how to listen carefully and patiently to other people. Teach us how to say what we have to say clearly, simply, and openly. Teach us what responsibility toward you and others really means.

■ Cut through all our egoism and self-interest, Jesus. Make us understand what patriotism must mean in one world of conflicting nationalisms. Educate us to support the United Nations and other international organizations which bring people together in a shared sense of human concern. Work with us, Lord, to bridge gulfs and divisions between nations and persons.

What can I do about war and peace?

■ I mean, how can I do anything which will affect the power structures which hold the key to basic decisions about waging war or maintaining peace? I've marched in peace demonstrations, fasted in protest against nuclear experiments, signed petitions, and tried seriously to study the issues involved. But what have I been able to accomplish?

■ I know we can't pass over this situation, yet we are somehow supposed to live with the outrage of doing exactly that.

■ I see the beauty of your creation, and am grateful, but then I see in my mind's eye the very real possibility of its destruction. How can I stand this, Jesus? What is prayer supposed to mean if I am passively accepting a peril which it is sinful to accept? I don't want to misuse prayer to lull me about this crisis, Lord. I want to accept my responsibility of cooperating with you in the continuing and present act of creation. How can I do it?

Three young children died in that room

■ It's just a room in a slum, in a big American city, but when a fire started it became a very special room, a death chamber for three youngsters.

■ They tell me eleven people have died in this area of a few blocks, Jesus. All died in fires when they were trapped and couldn't get out. The people in the area can't move away because there's no place for them to go.

■ It doesn't seem fair for some people to have nice homes with safety, Lord, while other people can't get out of a slum like this except in a coffin.

It takes away my guilt when I blame your murder on the Jews, Jesus

■ Why should I feel guilty about it? I wasn't there. If I had been, I can't imagine myself shouting anything about crucifying you.

■ The Roman soldiers were there, of course, along with Pontius Pilate. And the Jews were there, the Sanhedrin and those who cried for Barabbas instead of you.

■ I wasn't there, Jesus. I had nothing to do with it.

■ I *was* there, Jesus, as you know. I am a part of mankind, although I like to remember it only when I want something from my brother or society at large, and like to forget it when it involves me in humanness outside myself.

■ I shouted for your crucifixion, Jesus. I taunted you as you bore your cross, and I stood in the crowd to watch you die.

■ I did this again just today, Jesus.

■ Forgive me. I ask for your mercy and forgiveness. But how can I ask forgiveness of Jews, after the pogroms, burnings, genocide, every form of discrimination, and most of it in your name? In your own humanity, you were a Jew. I am involved in your murder, Jesus, as in the lives and deaths of countless Jews. I ask forgiveness of you for the guilt I share in the deaths of Jews murdered by Christians in your name, for the guilt I share in the countless persecutions of Jews by Christians in your name.

■ I am shamed. I am mute.

Prayers for Racial Freedom

Blacks and whites make me angry, Lord

■ Why does it make any difference to some of us? For Christ's sake, why does it, Lord? Why do people get their backs up about this color bit?

■ I got very mad at a white guy today, Lord, when he came out with all the old clichés during a conversation we were having. He just sat there with a damned grin on his face and started telling the old lies about Negroes. He never raised his voice. He was always a gentleman, you know, very respectable and proper, while he crucified Negroes; I felt the nails driven into me, too. I wanted to slug him, Lord, and smash his mask. I wanted to find out what was really behind it.

■ I don't know what to do at times like that. I'm supposed to be patient and long-suffering, but I become angry, Jesus, *angry*.

■ And the other day I got mad at a Negro. He was so ashamed of being a Negro that he had stopped being human. When I reached out to him for a human response he just burrowed farther inside his brown skin and wouldn't come out.

■ He smiled all the time, too, Jesus, like a smiling dead man, rotting behind this mask.

■ I know you've done a lot to wise us up, Lord, but please keep on trying. You've even given your own self to wise us up. But, Jesus, please don't give up on us.

■ Please get through to the smiling white man and the smiling Negro. And get through to me, please get through to me. Who is each of us really, Jesus? Are we black and white, or are we human? They say I'm white, and sometimes black, Lord, but what do *you* say about me, and about all of us?

I find it very difficult to pray in this situation

■ It seems to me we have all prayed a long time about situations like this, yet have done little or nothing to change them. Maybe we thought prayer was magic, Jesus, and decided we didn't need to cooperate actively with you in working for a better world.

■ What are we to say, Lord, about this family that lives in a wooden shack here on a winding dirt road in Mississippi? The father, a Negro laborer, earns less than a thousand dollars a year under the modern slavery of "the plantation system." The mother is now bearing their seventh child. The family is hungry. As I see it, these persons have no opportunity to break out of the grinding, desperate life in which they have been prisoners since birth.

■ Lots of well-fed, comfortable, middle-class people everywhere are praying for "situations" like this all the time. But they don't seem to do enough about changing such situations by altering political and economic facts of life, or helping specific men, women, and children who are victims.

■ Isn't prayer expressed in action, Jesus, and isn't real action a form of prayer? Then maybe people in Chicago ought to pray for "situations" like this by getting involved in Chicago community organization efforts and in the lives of Chicago victims; perhaps people in Boston, London, São Paolo, and Johannesburg ought to pray in this way too. And people in Mississippi.

■ Otherwise, wouldn't it be more honest not to go through the mere motions of praying, Lord? I mean, if we do not intend to offer ourselves and cooperate with you in fighting evil?

I see white and black, Lord

■ I see white teeth in a black face.

■ I see black eyes in a white face.

■ Help us to see *persons,* Jesus—not a black person or a white person, a red person or a yellow person, but human persons.

How may the heart be taught, Jesus?

■ When a mind is closed and communication has ceased, how may a person be reached? If his heart has never learned to love, or has stopped loving, how may the heart be taught, Jesus?

He's a black boy, Jesus. Will he learn to be a man?

■ He's not yet ten years old, Jesus. He's a Negro child in Alabama.

■ Today he saw a white man strike his father in the face. His father could not defend himself without being attacked by a group of white men, so he just stood there silently and took it.

■ The young child was silent, too, Lord, for a moment. Then he started to cry. He screamed in a terrible shame and fear, not just because his father had suffered pain, but because his father's manhood had been attacked and his life diminished.

■ I remember how you were taken out and lynched, Jesus, so you know the agony of rejection, separation between persons, and murder. What is the relation between your own lynching and crucifixion, Lord, and this boy who cries out as you did from the cross?

Why won't they let him be himself, Lord?

■ Negroes call him an Uncle Tom, and whites say he is a member of the "black bourgeoisie."

■ He just wants to be himself. He's quite secure in his family life, and his wife is a very strong and loving person, but the labels other people give him make him self-conscious. Sometimes he feels guilty, guilty to be considered a Negro instead of a "nigger," a "white Negro" instead of a Negro.

■ He lives in a white neighborhood. He works in a white office. His wife and children have white friends. He's angry, much of the time, about Negro second-class citizenship, but his job is one that gives him a chance to do something about civil rights.

■ Why can't people just let him be himself, instead of making him into a category?

They hate everything white

■ They're young Negroes who were brought up to consider white beautiful and black ugly. They never received an education in Negro history or culture, especially in terms of African origins and Negro contributions to American history. They were taught they had to make it in a white world in a white way.

■ They grew up believing they were somehow inferior, because that's what white people, and a number of Negroes, made them believe.

■ Now they're mad, Lord, because they have learned they were taught lies. They know they're black—and also completely human and fully citizens, yet without authentic freedom or full civil rights. They don't want any part of white values, which, in the light of their experience, seem to be sick and corrupt. Now they feel white is ugly and black is beautiful. They just don't believe either white promises or white declarations about love and justice.

■ Where do all of us go from here—into one world or separate worlds? Is what *you* want going to be able to make any difference in what all of us do?

The so-called Christians have rejected her, Jesus

■ She is a schoolteacher, living in a large Northern city. In her experience, the church is a series of segregated private clubs rather than really your body on earth. She wants to worship with whites but has always been made to feel unwelcome by them.

■ The white Christians, she has learned, want to live in segregated white neighborhoods. When she has looked for an apartment, they have insulted her, lied to her, or politcly told her they don't want Negro tenants.

■ She has tried very hard to live in a society as a person who is Negro, rather than a Negro who is not really considered a person. What kind of Christianity, trading on your name, can deny her human rights and her full membership in your body on earth?

A litany for racial unity

■ O God the Father, our Father, who created man in your own image and after your own likeness, so that we are all sons of God who are loved equally by you and share equally the privilege of having been created in your own image,
Have mercy upon us.

■ O God the Son, Jesus Christ, the Word of God, who died on the cross for us, to release us from the terrifying power of sin and death, and to save us from the hell of separation from God and from each other,
Have mercy upon us.

■ O God the Holy Spirit, the presence with us of holy God, the sovereign and sanctifier of our individual and social lives, the healing power sent to infuse our hate with love and to bind up the wounds of the social body and of the spirit,
Have mercy upon us.

■ Judge us not for our self-love, our rationalizations and lies in our relations with other men, our perpetuation of social and psychological ghettos in which to barricade ourselves from our brothers, our maintenance of segregation as our national and religious way of life, and our too easy acceptance of cultural norms because we wish to be popular, therefore becoming conformist in our thoughts and actions,
Spare us, good Lord.

■ We petition you to hear us, so that your Spirit will convert our intention, and we may cease being racial hypocrites and may commit ourselves to the cause of social justice which represents the working of love in the sphere of human life,

We ask you to hear us, Lord.

■ That you will teach us really to see one another, not in racial categories or as strangers wearing colored masks but as living and human persons created by you in your very image,

We ask you to hear us, Lord.

■ That you will endow us with courage to fight against racial evil in the spirit of nonviolence and love, making no peace with the oppression of this injustice,

We ask you to hear us, Lord.

■ That you will inform our minds and enlighten our ignorance so that we may do battle with evil in all those specific social and economic situations which limit another person's opportunities to work, study, vote, live, cultivate freedom, and pursue happiness,

We ask you to hear us, Lord.

■ That you will let us hear the human hearts beating alongside our own, and let others hear the messages of our own beating hearts, so that we may communicate with one another in a spirit of compassion and naked mutual need,

We ask you to hear us, Lord.

■ That you will show us how to avoid empty smiles and polite forms which perpetuate evasion of truth and dishonest relationships,
We ask you to hear us, Lord.

■ That you will look with mercy upon those who have been broken in body, mind, or spirit as fighters in the cause of racial integration and human love; upon those who have been imprisoned or are now in jails for this cause; upon those who have seen loved ones martyred in lynchings, murder, and humiliations; and upon those who have been martyrs themselves,
We ask you to hear us, Lord.

■ That you will lift up in spirit those who have been subject to loss of employment, to social criticism and isolation, and to personal pain because of their involvement in the struggle for social justice and human love; and those who have witnessed to their belief in your creation of man in your own image by participation in expressions of protest against injustice and inhumanity,
We ask you to hear us, Lord.

■ That you will instruct the hearts of those who actively hate in human relations, who are ignorant owing to their education or background, who keep alive the power of prejudice, and who are persecutors, jailers, racist leaders of public opinion, racist educators, priests, rabbis, and ministers,
We ask you to hear us, Lord.

■ That you will guide us in a resolute advance in interracial efforts to combat the evils of racial segregation, so that we may avoid the intensified and subtle forms of continued segregation which isolated racial efforts by themselves can represent; that we—white and black, red and yellow—may be united rather than separated in the common fight for equality, justice, and humanity under God,
We ask you to hear us, Lord.

■ That you will gird us for the battle which we must wage against the forces of racial discrimination and segregation which deny both your holiness in your act of creation and the humanness of man in his having been created by you; that you will save us from self-righteousness, increase humility in us, call us to love you and one another, and so possess our bodies, minds, and spirits by your spirit that we may heed the call to do your will in our lives, and have the strength to carry it out in the world,
We ask you to hear us, Lord.

■ That we may be enabled to offer to you, for your blessing, the totality of our lives and each others' lives, including our colors or our lack of colors,
We ask you to hear us, Lord.

■ That we may be given strength and love to accept Christian tension in the midst of unchristian peace, and to seek that peace which passes all understanding in the midst of the Christian's war,
We ask you to hear us, Lord.

■ O God—you who are neither red, yellow, black, nor white, but who has created us in a marvelous variety of rich colors and marked us with your image,
We ask you to hear us, Lord.

All: Our Father, who is in heaven, hallowed be your name. Your kingdom come, your will be done, on earth as it is in heaven. Give us this day our daily bread. And forgive us our trespasses, as we forgive those who trespass against us. And lead us not into temptation, but deliver us from evil. For yours is the kingdom, and the power, and the glory, for ever and ever. Amen.

Lord, arise, help us, and deliver us for your Name's sake.

■ Glory be to the Father, and to the Son, and to the Holy Spirit.

As it was in the beginning, is now, and ever shall be, world without end. Amen.

■ The grace of Our Lord Jesus Christ, and the love of God, and the fellowship of the Holy Spirit, be with us all evermore. Amen.

Prayers in the City

They're in a golden world, Jesus

■ They're having a party in a hotel suite which is elegant and located in the best hotel in the heart of the city. There's music, jewelry, glamour, gin, V.I.P. status, and POWER, Lord.

■ But nobody's having any fun. They're too busy sparring with one another in the POWER game which, tonight, is also the sex-and-booze tournament.

■ Everybody looks slick and, underneath tans and wigs, somewhat lonely. I mean, they're not relating, Jesus. They're only observing the stiff protocol of small talk and ground rules. This informal gathering is as rigid as the court of Louis XIV, only the accents here are of Detroit, Houston, and Los Angeles.

■ The masks are on parade tonight, Jesus. The masks are smiling and laughing to cover up status anxieties and bleeding ulcers.

■ Tell us about freedom, Jesus.

It's a jazz spot, Jesus

■ He's a jazz musician who works here. Jazz for him is art and life, Lord. This is the way he expresses himself, tells it as it is, hangs on, and climbs.

■ But the night-club world is a tough one if you want to be free and be yourself. It's interested in top stars and pop performers. Steady work and the buck go together, and both are somewhat elusive. At least, that's his experience.

■ It's late in here tonight, Jesus. The customers are listening over their drinks; they're getting scared because soon they'll have to go into the dark night outside. There won't be any music or Scotch or lights out there on the early-morning street. If there was someplace to go, they'd leave, but this is the last place open.

■ The musician is wondering if they're hearing him at all through all their listening. He has something to say, and he's saying it. It's about death and life, sex and hunger, knowing yourself and being known, the dream, the vision. He's looking at the people, right into their dead and alive eyes, and he wants them to hear him.

■ Does he know you hear him, Lord?

Look up at that window, Lord, where the old guy is sitting

■ See, he's half-hidden by the curtain that's moving a little in the breeze. That tenement—it's a poor place to have to live, isn't it, Jesus?

■ He is seated alone by a kitchen table and looking blankly out the window. He lives with his sister, who is away working all day. There is nothing for him to do. He doesn't have any money; all he has is time.

■ Who is he in *my* life, Jesus? What has he got to do with me? He's your brother, and you love him. What does this say to me, Lord? I don't know what sense I am supposed to make out of this. I mean, how can I possibly be responsible in any honest, meaningful way for that guy?

■ He just moved a short bit away from the window. Maybe he moved because he felt my eyes on him from the sidewalk down here. I didn't mean to embarrass him, Lord; I just wanted to let him know somebody understands he's alive and he's your brother, so he's not alone or lost. Does he know it, Jesus?

The kids are smiling, Jesus, on the tenement stoop

■ The little girl is the oldest, and she's apparently in charge of the younger two, her brothers.

■ But suddenly she's crying and her two brothers are trying to comfort her. Now everything seems to be peaceful, and she's smiling again.

■ But what's ahead for them, Lord? Home is this broken-down dump on a heartless, tough street. What kind of a school will they go to? Will it be hopelessly overcrowded? Will it be a place that breeds despair? Will it change these kids' happy smiles into angry, sullen masks they'll have to wear for the rest of their lives?

■ I look at their faces and realize how they are our victims, especially when we like to say they are beautiful children, but we don't change conditions which will make their faces hard and their hearts cynical.

■ Have these kids got a chance, Jesus? Will they know anything about dignity or love or health? Jesus, looking at these kids, I'm afraid for them and for all of us.

The old house is nearly all torn down, Lord

■ What became of the people who used to live here? Where are they now, and what has happened to the roots they had here?

■ The demolition men are doing a good job. A week ago they started cold, and now the house is just about down. I saw them taking it down floor by floor, room by room. They tied a rope onto the wooden frames of rooms and pulled them, bringing them tumbling down onto the ground. Suddenly the derelict old house is nearly gone. In a day or so there will be only a patch of ground on a city block where new people were born, couples made love, men and women fought and relaxed and worked, and death visited from time to time. It will be strange for people who used to live there when they come back home and there isn't any home.

■ Help us to learn how to live with mobility and rapid change and the absence of old securities, remembering that you didn't have any place to lay your head when you were living among us as a man.

In this ugly red building, old people are waiting for death

■ They're inside, Jesus, two or three in a room, and three times a day other people bring them food to eat. Otherwise, they generally don't have anything to do except watch television sometimes.

■ Is this death for them now, Jesus? Do they know they will have life afterward, when they die? Their families must hate to come and see them in this ugly old house, Lord—is that why they hardly ever do?

■ But these old people in this old house—are they happy at all? Do they know you're in there with them and also that you have overcome the power and loneliness of death? Do they? I hope the doctors who come there to see them have a lot of patience and kindness, and that the nurses do too. Help everybody in that house to have a lot of patience and kindness, Jesus.

I know pity is useless, Lord, but I can't help feeling sorry for her

■ She still has more writing talent than a dozen other people, but her life is going down the drain. She never learned how to live with her talent or use it. She starts drinking, and, when she gets tired of that, she takes heroin. She ran through most of the men in her life a long time ago.

■ But she always gives everybody that bright, energetic smile as if nothing was the matter, and she doesn't eat her heart out until she is alone. Her smile isn't jaded—she has a quality of innocence which is very real.

■ She gives with the assured patter she learned when she was enrolled in the best schools. She still wears clothes like the debutante she was fifteen years ago, although she has become very heavy and her coat is a rag. She lives in a run-down house in a rough neighborhood. Her family is ashamed of her now and doesn't want anything to do with her.

■ Be good to her, please, Lord. She is so insecure and lost and needs your love badly. Of all your mixed-up loved ones, she is one of the saddest, even though she always wears this big smile. Jesus, underneath her tired, worn-out mask, let her know she is loved.

He'll never work again, Jesus

■ He's sitting there on the park bench and is just beginning to quit fighting the fact. He's only around forty, and he's had it because he doesn't have a skill and automation has come.

■ But he's not making any sense out of all this, Lord. His wife goes off to work in the mornings as a domestic, and the two kids are in school; the other one is in the service.

■ Instead of being the leader of his family he's nothing, Jesus, nothing at all. He can sit at home and look at television, but that gets boring; anyway, he's a man and wants to be a man. When his wife brings home the money she earns he's belligerent, and takes some of it to buy booze so he can black out and forget for a little while.

■ The kids despise him. When he pulls rank with them, he feels less like a man or a human being than at any other time. He feels left out of things, forgotten, a human hulk in a bright, flashing world of machines and successful men. The sheen of success isn't on him, Lord. He looks seedy and tired and washed out.

■ What is he to do, Jesus? What is his family to do? What am I to do, standing here, looking on?

Everybody says he's going places, Lord

■ See him over there, Lord, driving the new blue car? He's in a hurry to get home so he can get ready to go out again.

■ He's always in a hurry, Lord. He knows what he wants and how to get it. His future in business is carefully mapped out. He's a young executive, and he lives in the right neighborhood, belongs to the right clubs, and attends the right church.

■ But he feels awfully threatened, Jesus, by a lot of things and people. He doesn't see why his world can't remain secure, old-fashioned, Protestant, and white. If some foreigners in Africa or Asia are causing trouble, he doesn't see why America doesn't really stand up to its enemies, because then there would be peace and security.

■ Reading the newspaper disturbs him. If only something could be done by the government about some of these problems—the spread of Communism, violence in our cities, black people claiming equality with whites—then he could see more point to his working so hard for security.

■ He's looking out of his car window. Does he see persons, or just things? Does he see you standing on the street, Jesus?

Prayers on the Campus

They say he's rocking the boat, Lord

■ He's considered too outspoken, and other faculty members say he's on the way out. The administration is nervous about his peace and civil rights activities. The university public relations man doesn't like to hear his name mentioned.

■ But he believes education involves making a commitment about life, and then acting on it no matter what it may cost. He's at war with some of his colleagues who seem, in his opinion, to hide behind words and avoid action.

■ He keeps risking his security by sticking his neck out on controversial issues. He says the university can't side-step such questions. Many students love him, but others feel he's a kook and don't understand why he can't settle down and do his routine job.

■ Please work with him in his restlessness, Lord. Give him all the interior peace that's possible without letting him go soft. Help him to pace himself in the fight, Jesus, and not to sell out under the pressures.

They thought they were in love, Jesus, before they had sex

■ He's a senior in college and she's a freshman, and last weekend they crawled into the sack together. I mean, all the barriers came down. Now they can't figure out what they should do.

■ They thought they were playing it cool, sleeping in the same room but not the same bed. And then, just before dawn, there they were in each other's arms.

■ She had made up her mind before not to go all the way with him, and, now that she has, she no longer understands herself. Her self-image is shaken. She says she did it because she loved him so much and still does.

■ The boy's image of her is shaken, too, because it demanded that she wait. He enjoyed having sex with her, but he now regards her as a stranger, maybe even a tramp. He can't reconcile the ideal image with the reality which his desire has produced. He says he's indifferent to her now.

■ How can sex shake people's lives so much, Jesus? What does it mean for love—now that they've "made love"? What *should* it mean for each of them, and for the two of them together?

They won't let him be a person, Lord

■ There are eight-nine Negroes out of six thousand students on the campus, Jesus, and John has decided the only way to survive is to play a role. He smiles when he is angry, he looks impassive when he would like to laugh, and he laughs when things get tense.

■ Some of the students resent his being at the university. Others go out of their way to be nice to him only because he's a Negro, and he dislikes these the most. He also has a white friend who betrays him sometimes without even being aware of it, just by going where John isn't welcome.

■ John dated a white girl a few times. He likes her, but the Dean of Women told her parents, and there was a big blow-up about it. He hasn't taken her out again even though she telephones him.

■ John's professors keep suggesting he write about Negro topics for term papers, and he isn't ever able to forget on the campus that he's kind of a token Negro, different from the other students.

■ He knows he has to make it, not just for himself but as a Negro in a white society. Will he ever be able to be himself in this world, Jesus?

She's a popular co-ed, but she doesn't know who she is

■ She's probably the most popular girl on the campus. She's certainly one of the best-looking, and she has a very real smile and seems completely secure, Jesus. You could hardly find anybody who dislikes her.

■ But she dislikes herself, or, at least, the self she feels she was handed but can't figure out. She thinks she must be two different selves, the operating one and another which is hidden under layers of complexity she can't get to. She wants to find out who that other self is because she believes she would like to be it. She simply doesn't know the self everybody seems to be relating to.

■ Everybody responds to her smile. She is tired of it and has come to feel it's a lie of some kind. She wants friends who would like that *other* self instead of this one which is a stranger—or enemy—to her.

■ The other night she broke up with the boy she likes. She cared too much about him to let him be hurt. She thought she should find out who she is before she lets anybody she cares about get too involved with *this* self. She wanted to love him with her other self, but didn't know how, or who that self might be.

■ Here she comes now, Lord, smiling her way across the campus. Help me to smile back—at her *other* self.

He has run out of steam, Jesus, and the students know it

■ He was considered one of the best men on the faculty a few years ago. He somehow found time then to talk to the students who wanted to see him, do his research, teach his classes, serve on his committees, and even complete his dissertation and get his tenure at the university.

■ Maybe he's just used up all his energy. He isn't on top of what's happening in his field any more. The students still feel he's a good teacher, but he's tough to get to see now. Even after you get into his office, he's preoccupied and doesn't seem involved with you. He resents the younger faculty members who are well liked and are doing a good job.

■ I don't know what's happened, or why he seems to have given up. One night at a faculty party he suddenly said something that sounded extremely bitter, as if he had gotten too sharp a look at the vanity of his intellectual pretensions and of the whole academic game.

■ Is this another case, Jesus, where you need to help someone accept his own mediocrity?

Suddenly he's out of the "in" group, Jesus

■ He had been earmarked, everybody said, for a top job in the college. His background was perfect, he had published, he was good with people, and he could raise important money.

■ It was, everybody said, a sure thing for him. A clique gathered around him. His wife knocked herself out playing the culture game, going everywhere with the right people.

■ Then everything seemed to go to pieces. He never knew exactly what happened. He was no longer "in" because another group got "in." His wife continued doing the right thing but at the wrong times. His publisher rejected the *big* book he had spent eight years getting finished.

■ Now he's in a fast blur that is passing him by. His wife is out tonight at a campus Little Theater opening. He is looking at television and has just poured himself another drink. The phone is ringing, but he doesn't answer it. He feels raw and bleeding, Jesus; he just wants peace, and not to be bothered any more. Who's going to show him that your peace means starting to care all over again?

She's asking you why she's so unattractive, Lord

■ Her parents made her feel their disappointment, and resented her withdrawal and apparent indifference to clothes and make-up. She's grown up without poise or outward security, and asks herself why she was born.

■ The other night a popular man on campus took her out. She couldn't believe he'd asked her for a date, but she spent a long time getting ready and was excited and pleased when he called for her.

■ He drove the car out into the country and demanded to have sex with her. He told her she wouldn't have any other good dates if she didn't, but, if she did, she could go out a lot.

■ When she refused, he insulted her and drove her straight back to her dormitory without speaking. She had thought he liked her. Now she feels like giving up and wishes she could die. There doesn't seem to be anything for her to look forward to.

■ Get her out of the hell she's in, Lord. She's got to understand that you find real beauty in her. Help us to provide the mirrors in which she can begin to see that beauty herself.

He doesn't think he can make it, Lord

■ He did a pretty good job of studying and making his grades in high school, but now he's at the university and scared stiff.

■ So he cheated on a big exam the other day because he thought he had to if he was going to get the grade he needed. Then he felt more confused than guilty, but his confidence has been hurt. He wonders now about the purpose of anything, and he's covering up his insecurity by being angry and wearing a chip on his shoulder.

■ If he doesn't make it, he has no idea what to do with his life. His family says everything depends on how he does at the university. But he's sure the only way he can make it is to cheat again. That seems a dead end because, when he does, he feels useless and very cheap inside.

■ Lord, show him how to be very cool and quiet, and let him start being honest with himself.

Meditations on Films

Sitting in the theater, I can scarcely wait for the lights to dim

■ Here I am in my anonymity. I feel shut off from every distraction. The screen is remote, *up there,* and I'm down here, able to relate or not relate to it as I choose.

■ The film has begun. It is telling a story, and concerns persons. Now I recognize myself. I'm up there, too, Jesus, involved in trying to make a decision. It's painful and I'm suffering.

■ I feel the closeness of other persons near me in the theater. I'm not suffering alone. We are so naked, Jesus, sitting here together and seeing ourselves (and each other) up there. Only the story isn't *up there* any more. It's *here.*

■ When the lights come up, and the movie has ended, will we remember anything of our closeness, Lord, or will we all be sitting quite alone? At first I wanted both escape and communion inside this theater. Now I know I can't escape, Jesus, and also how much I need communion.

"Citizen Kane"

■ Who is this Great Man, Jesus? I perceive his drive but can't understand it because it seems to destroy everyone, including himself. Yet he doesn't seem to want to be destroyed.

■ He can't seem to express his love (or is it raw need?) in simplicity to a single person. So the egoism builds up as a kind of panoply of compensation for a bottomless hurt. But what is this hurt which defies healing?

■ Looking at him, I see decadence and misuse of power overtaking hope and idealism. His death is the completion of a circle of unquenchable pain masked by, and fulfilled in, restlessness.

■ On his deathbed he whispers the name "Rosebud." This was the name painted on his childhood sled. Is there a name of absolutely private meaning in every man's life, Jesus? If we dig, can we find roots that may tell us who—and whose—we are?

"The Silence"

■ Bergman is telling me about the possibility of a breakdown in communication between persons. That sounds trite, but for me it becomes a study of life, in which you do not exist.

■ The tank is making its way through empty, silent city streets at night. It is frightening to me, Lord, as an image of dehumanized existence.

■ The man, after having sex with the woman, just stands in front of the hotel-room mirror combing his hair, Lord, while she tries to say something real to him about her feelings and doubts. He can't hear her at all.

■ Later, when the old man tries to tell the young boy about his life, showing him photographs of loved ones, the youngster escapes with the pictures and hides them underneath the hotel-corridor carpeting.

■ Lord, a man has to be able to do something with his feelings and ideas, he has to try to give them to somebody and try to share his own understanding of himself and life. What happens when all hope of this is completely cut off?

■ Help us, Jesus, all of us, to reach each other and to go on trying even when it seems hopeless.

"Zorba the Greek"

■ I'm set on fire by who Zorba is and how he reacts to life, Lord. He lives life. He beholds the earth, smells and feels it, and finds it good.

■ I suppose he's no saint. I'm not sure, Jesus, what it means to be a saint right now. (I don't think it means to act "saintly." I'm afraid that kind of thing is why people are bored with "religion.") I mean, Zorba is *human,* Lord, and he does good and bad human things. But he seems to love life, bounces back from disasters, meets other people's needs, and gets involved in their lives and all of life that comes his way.

■ Isn't life, for Zorba, something to be celebrated as being holy? Do you yourself, Jesus, label some things in life as "holy," and others as "profane"? I don't think you do, but so many people who call themselves Christians seem to ignore you completely when they set up their blue laws and censorship boards.

■ Zorba's dance of life is a wonderful dialogue with you, Jesus. Teach me to dance too, or, at least, to be free with you, and to understand how newness of life and renewal are stronger than death.

"Hulot's Holiday"

■ This strikes me as ludicrous and true, Jesus. Fey abandon seems to run counterpoint to a formal charade, and an insane melody plays in the background.

■ There is gibberish and utter absurdity, but beneath all this there is Hulot himself with all his humanness. His gait sets in motion a hilarious reaction from the audience, but, to Hulot, it is simply his natural way of movement.

■ Is seriousness always just a stone's throw away from slapstick, Lord? Is there a touch of foolishness in all of life so that, after all, natural self-satire is the most telling?

■ Why, then, can't we laugh with more fun at ourselves, Jesus? Why are we so humorless and serious—and so hard on ourselves?

"Nothing But A Man"

■ Here is a film in which I learn something about effort. I mean real effort, not just the phony stereotype of it with artificial sweat.

■ I mean, this guy could so easily not only have given up, Lord, he could have wrecked three lives, one of them being his own. But he didn't and he stayed—quite sensibly, maturely, it seems to me—in the fight to be himself, a human being, a person, a man.

■ He is beaten down, Lord, by every force and circumstance around him, but he stays human. He doesn't become a category or a thing for the sake of making it. He gambles making it on his resolution to be a man.

■ Thus, at the end, he walks back not only into love and responsibility but also squarely into the face of bigotry and hate. He is in danger because, in his small Southern town, he won't be a "good nigger." He will be nothing but a man. Help us to get the message in this, Jesus, not only about others but for ourselves.

"Nobody Waved Goodbye"

■ He is a teenager and he's fleeing, Jesus. Alone in a stolen car, he is crying, blinded by the night lights on a great expressway.

■ His girl, pregnant and alone, has left him. His parents can only show their disappointment that he's not going to the university and being what they want. Peter wanted his life to be go-go-go, but it wouldn't cooperate. All he could do was make certain rejections without being able to find positive affirmations to put in their place.

■ Why did Peter come so far in his rebellion, Lord? It seems to me he was sure there was some place to go. This showed in his eyes, his whole manner, his exuberant restlessness. And he believed there was enough security inside himself.

■ He's one of society's misfits, not one of its shining knights. But he can't understand any of this at all, how it happened and what it means. He's been humbled, kicked, debased, and he couldn't find any bounce anywhere.

■ There is a terrible sense of waste, of human dead ends. The boy keeps shifting from shrill conversational heights to a winning naïveté and quick unreachable assertions of ego. But in his own way he has been looking, often quite honestly, for alternatives to a style of life he didn't want. The film doesn't judge; he just couldn't find any alternatives that made sense or seemed to work for him.

■ But how is Peter going to see that there are other possibilities, Jesus? What if he thinks he's seen it all already?

"Breathless"

■ There is no sentiment here, Jesus, except in the tough guy who mugs a victim in a men's room. But he proves to be a patsy for a girl who tests her lovelessness intellectually by turning her lover in to the police.

■ In this film, Jesus, a new toughness with a tenderness beneath its senseless cruelty seems to meet the sexy shrug without a future. Boy kills, boy meets girl and takes her to bed, boy is betrayed by girl, boy dies looking up at girl from the street and softly calling her a "little bitch," girl looks down at boy, saying nothing.

■ Yet these two had known each other intimately. Why were their interior lives unrelated to their exterior lives, their motions and actions, Lord? Why were they afraid of, or unfamiliar with, compassion?

"La Strada"

■ What are strength and weakness?

■ He is so weak, despite his playing a Strong Man in a circus. She has an inner strength of grace and humor, yet she is very small and weak when he beats her.

■ He can't seem to control his feelings, Lord, so he flails out at other persons when he is really hating himself. Does he feel very inadequate and afraid of relationship, underneath his toughness and brawn? It is evident that he needs tenderness, along with a savage need for its return, but he is confused and embarrassed by these feelings. In fact, they bring out a singular crudeness and hostility in him.

■ She needs an assurance of love and purpose which he is unable to give her. After her death, for which he is responsible, he crouches by the sea at night. He cries, his heart breaking at the realization of who he is, and what he has done.

■ Will he be able to find the lost self-image of his creation, Lord? Can he put together the pieces of life in your image of grace, or must he remain a broken victim of violence and despair?

Prayers for Sexual Freedom

This young girl got pregnant, Lord, and she isn't married

■ There was this guy, you see, and she had had a little too much to drink. It sounds so stupid, but the loneliness was real. Where were her parents in all this? It's hard to know. For the girl, they probably seemed indifferent, absorbed in their familiar routines, uninterested in her real life. But did she ever try to tell them about it? And would they have listened?

■ Now the guy doesn't want anything to do with her; he's tied up in some job and is very busy. He's especially annoyed about the idea of the child and wonders why she didn't know better. He thought she understood what the rules were: a girl doesn't have to get pregnant these days if she doesn't want to.

■ The girl is sitting across from me now, so cool and collected. She can't even admit to herself how hurt she is, and goes on analyzing the situation with bits of freshman psychology. And meanwhile there's a new life growing inside her, making new demands on her; does the textbook have an answer to that?

■ There's nothing ahead for her with the guy. She tells me he's really in love with somebody else. She's not in love with anyone; she's sure of that. And she's honest enough to admit, even knowing what she does now, that she'd go back to sleeping with the guy. Does she really think that's all she needs? She admits she's thought of suicide, but says she doesn't have the strength to make any real decision, let alone that one.

■ What am I going to tell her, Jesus? How can I help her understand the nature of the love she's looking for?

They've been married for twenty years, Jesus, and they say they hate each other

■ They want a divorce—that's the one thing they're sure of. Not that either of them is in love with anyone else. There just doesn't seem to be much love in the whole situation. Was it simply sex that brought them together, and sex that is killing them now?

■ They keep accusing each other of long-standing infidelities, and tell you they would have broken up long ago except for the children, but the children seem merely weapons to be used against each other. And then, when they've finally decided—once again—to make a real break, they end up in bed together at 4 A.M., and everything is fine until the next evening, when they feel it's time for a final break again.

■ They've hurt each other so terribly; no marriage counselor can undo what they've worked at so long. They've been to the psychiatrist and the minister and anyone else who would listen, with or without being paid for it, but no one knows how hate and love get so mixed up with each other. Or wasn't there any love here, Lord, ever?

■ Where do sex and love come together in these two lives? Should they try to make it alone or together? Can they make it together, Jesus? Can they make it alone?

This is a homosexual bar, Jesus

■ It looks like any other bar on the outside, only it isn't. Men stand three and four deep at this bar—some just feeling a sense of belonging here, others making contacts for new sexual partners.

■ This isn't very much like a church, Lord, but many members of the church are also here in this bar. Quite a few of the men here belong to the church as well as to this bar. If they knew how, a number of them would ask you to be with them in both places. Some of them wouldn't, but won't you be with them, too, Jesus?

He's a married man, Lord, but he says he doesn't feel married

■ He's twenty-five years old, and he thinks he loves his wife, but he says he can't talk to her. "I have satisfactory sex with her," he says, "and I'm not mad at her, but I don't know why we're living together."

■ Underneath his words, what is he really saying, Jesus? He goes on about not feeling alive, but he can't seem to explain why he's fed up with marriage. "I've asked my wife to get a job and become financially independent so we can get a divorce."

■ He doesn't seem cruel or callous. He has two handsome children and he seems fond enough of them. Was he forced to settle down too soon? What kind of impossible demands is he making of life that he can't work out his needs within his present situation?

■ I find myself wanting to shake him, maybe partly because he stays so even-tempered, soft-spoken, low-key. The kids drift in and he can see on my face all the old clichés about broken homes and children needing fathers and mothers together. He smiles gently, and I know I've muffed it; I'm not going to get through to him.

■ He's lived twenty-five years, but I'm not

sure what anything means to him yet. His wife obviously doesn't mean enough, and neither do his children.

■ Can you get past his defenses, Lord?

They are a couple in love, Jesus, but think they can't afford marriage yet

■ He is twenty-one, she is nineteen. They have been having sex together two or three times a week for two years. Now he has found that she hasn't been enjoying the sex but has been pretending to. "She feels guilty because we aren't married," the young man says. "What can we do? If we can't have a healthy sex life together, I'll call the whole thing off."

■ She accuses herself because she knows she went after him in the first place. She doesn't mention marriage to him, even though she would be more than happy to work to support him while he stayed in school. She even realizes that her very attitude of acceptance may be an unfair pressure on him.

■ Can they make something out of their situation, Lord? They're at least trying to talk to each other. The boy is smart enough to know that this problem is more than not having enough money, and is willing to admit that his pride has been hurt.

■ Take their mutual honesty, Lord, and work with it.

This man and woman are afraid of sex and each other and living

■ They are an attractive couple, Jesus. They have a number of friends and go out a good deal socially.

■ They have a double bed but have not engaged in sex together for more than two years. "This sex thing is ridiculous," she says, and goes on to insist she will visit her attorney on Monday morning to break up their marriage. But she doesn't.

■ They drink too much and have many arguments, but they do this privately. It isn't only their sexual needs they cannot meet, Lord. They are close to each other, yet very far apart in many ways. They remember each other's birthday, they are grateful for past kindnesses and share a deep concern for each other's welfare. But what holds them together more than anything else is the fear of aloneness and a kind of pity. Each of them would be afraid to start over again with someone else; they would be too vulnerable in a new relationship.

■ So, they're just coasting on what they have, and losing themselves more and more in emptiness. They prefer never to stay at home but go to openings, smart resorts, and the "right" restaurants, hiding in the crowd that always provides a gala stage for the daily round of life. They need to give up their escapes, Jesus, and turn to each other in a mutual confession of need. Lord, let them look into each other's mirrors and each other's hearts.

They are called an interracial couple, Lord

■ What is that supposed to mean? He is a man, she is a woman, they love each other and are married. He is Negro, she is white.

■ But the rest of us have a way of making life quite difficult for them. We are color-conscious, so we stare at them. Some of us are racists, so we hate them.

■ Their marriage is a good one. Their baby, who doesn't belong to either a white or a black ghetto, seems to have an excellent chance of being free in an emerging new society.

■ Are we going to let this couple be free by accepting them, not on color lines but as a man and a woman who have become husband and wife?

She's a career girl involved with a married man

■ She meets him at her apartment when he lies to his wife about why he's not at home.

■ What does she expect to find in this brief encounter, Jesus? She experiences a searing, sweet, romantic coming-together with a time limit. She expresses a certain naked, hungry need to pour out her bottled-up life. Yet he has told her he is happily married and does not intend to leave his wife.

■ She wonders, more and more, What does it mean to "make love"? The goodbyes she has to say, and accept, are cool and brittle ones. She asks herself if the final goodbye won't be a tersely bitten-off ending of an incident that seemed to jab like a needle seeking blood.

■ How much hurt can she stand, Jesus? Does she realize that this style of searching leads to hurts and dead ends? Help her to understand what a full sexual union involves in terms of human relationship.

Meditations on the Cross

Help us really to dig in, Jesus, and be with you

■ After all the poor fiction and cheap biblical movies which have turned your life and death into almost bizarre superstition, Jesus, it's hard for me to see your cross as it really was.

■ They've even turned Jerusalem into such a tourist attraction that it's not at all easy, even while walking along the actual ground you walked, to visualize anything with honesty or accuracy.

■ I imagine it was sweaty and hot. When you said from the cross, "I thirst," I am sure you were very thirsty. It's easy for us today to say you were really thirsting for men's souls (and I'm sure you were), but isn't this just a dodge that keeps us from accepting the fact of your humanity? Why do we want to forget that you were a man, hanging on the cross for hours, who simply needed something to drink?

■ Can we somehow get through all the decoration which has been developed about the cross and just be quiet and be there with you?

Thanks for what you did about success and failure

■ Jesus, you ruined all the phony success stories forever when you didn't come down from the cross, turn your crown of thorns into solid gold, transform the crowd at Golgotha into a mighty army, march on Rome, and become *the king.*

■ Now every success symbol looks so shoddy and short-lived when it is placed over against your cross. You accepted and overcame death. You showed us the dimension of life in God's eternal dispensation which makes the careers we plan and the standards we accept look absurd.

■ When you refused to play the role of a Great Man, or the ultimate Big Shot, you really made us level with you as yourself, Lord.

Why is reality about you so shocking to us, Lord?

■ They've made the cross you hung on so pretty, Jesus.

■ I know the real cross wasn't pretty at all. But I guess I understand why they want to make copies of it out of fine woods and even semi-precious stones, because *you* hung on it.

■ Yet doesn't this romanticize your death, Lord, and give it a kind of gloss it didn't have? Your death was bloody and dirty and very real. Can't we face it that way, Jesus? And can't we face the fact that you were a real man, living a human life as well as God?

What is love, Jesus?

■ It seems so important, Jesus, that you called on the Father to forgive your torturers because, as you put it, they didn't know what they were doing.

■ But you kept on loving, even then.

■ Help us to learn from you, Lord, how to keep on loving when we feel like hating. It's hard. Some of us have even turned your cross into a symbol of hate. When the Ku Klux Klan burns a cross, Lord, the blasphemy of it startles me. Doesn't this mean, in a very real sense, joining the ranks of your own executioners?

■ Nevertheless, you were actively, creatively, responsibly *loving,* even on the cross, Jesus. Help us to see that love for what it is—in all its fierce passion and sweep of forgiveness.

You're hanging on a cross again, Jesus

■ The symbol is so familiar to us that maybe we don't think about the reality any more. Wasn't it simply the means of your execution, something like an electric chair or hangman's noose would be today?

■ In churches the cross always seems to be everywhere, over altars and in stained-glass windows and even hanging in clergymen's offices. I know it represents the act of redemption, but your whole life seems to do this much more significantly.

■ Is your death more important to us than your life, Lord? Is your death more central than your resurrection? Help us to keep these things in balance so that we don't lose sight of you among all the religious symbols we put up in your honor.

Help us to understand, Jesus, your pain and your prayer

■ On the cross, when you asked God why he had forsaken you, what did you really mean?

■ Were you reciting an old psalm or were you actually conscious of having been forgotten by God in a terribly painful and lost moment of time?

■ People have said this moment represented the depth of your agony on the cross, a spiritual crucifixion within the physical crucifixion. They have said your mental anguish was fused here with your bodily torture.

■ Yet you cried out to God. You never felt totally cut off from your Father. To me this has always seemed the deepest level of your dialogue with God, your deepest prayer.

■ Help me to know what you meant here, Lord.

Teach us the path, show us the way

■ They say that everyone has his own cross to bear, Lord. And you once said, "Take up your cross and follow me." What do these things mean? I think they mean that every person ultimately has to face up to reality—face his own destiny, his own calling, his own nature and responsibilities.

■ In your own life, Jesus, you faced reality directly and unequivocally. You incarnated the truth as you believed it. You didn't pander to any easy or obvious popularity. You attacked the hypocrisies of the human power structure head on. You rejected the *status quo* in favor of obedience to the Kingdom of God. And when it came to taking the consequences, you didn't shy away from the most difficult forms of torture and execution.

■ The way of the cross was your understanding of your mission and your faithfulness to it.

■ The way of the cross seems to be, for every individual Christian, the reality which dictates his style of life, defines his own mission, and brings him into communion with you.

■ Help me bear my cross on the way of the cross, Jesus.

■ Prayers on Traditional Themes

Grace at mealtime

■ Thank you for this food, Lord, thank you. We're grateful that we can eat when we're hungry. We're also happy and grateful that we can do it together and not be alone, without each other or you.

■ Nourish our bodies and minds as well as our souls. Make us stronger, especially in our wills, so that we can serve you and others instead of just asking favors for ourselves.

■ Show us the real needs of others, Jesus. You told us that when we do anything to any of your brothers—and ours—in the world, we actually do it to you. When, Lord, do we pass you by because we pass by one of our brothers who is in need? Teach us to see your face, Jesus, when we look into our brothers' faces.

■ Thank you for this knowledge of you and our brothers. Thank you for energy and strength, mercy and love.

■ Amen.

To Christ at Christmas

■ Why do we celebrate your birth but not your life?

■ Why do we call ourselves after your name but refuse to follow after your life?

■ I see your face, Jesus, in the face of a Negro woman in Mississippi whose life is made a hell by white "Christians." I see your face, Jesus, in the face of a lonely man in a crowded city. I see your face, Jesus, as loved and unloved in the faces of people who hate and the persons who love.

■ Christmas is a great mystery to me. (The way we practice it, is it a mystery to you, too?)

■ Through the sham and simplicity, the cruelty and joy, the exploitation and adoration of it, I see your face. Bless us, *us, us,* your brothers and sisters, your disciples, the humanity you died on the cross to redeem.

■ Thank you, Christ, on the occasion of Christmas and always, for giving us life in the midst of death, *life, life,* with you.

Invocation for a service organization

■ God our Father:

■ First, we pray that this may not be merely a superficial outward form of prayer to which we give a respectable attention that we believe is socially proper, yet may actually ignore or even rebuke as a mere outward form drained of inner dynamic and honest, radical meaning.

■ Second, we offer thanks for the love ethic you have given us, and for all social justice, nonviolence, and peace, wherever these are found and particularly where they indicate active opposition to injustice and false peace.

■ Third, we ask for your judgment upon immoral systems which pervert the law to serve their own unjust ends, as in the case of the Nazis in their persecution of Jews, in all totalitarian persecution of faith and education, and in any racial discrimination toward persons to whom you have given different colors of skin.

■ Have mercy upon us. Unite us in the common cause of social justice, in worship which is dynamically related to life, and in the upholding of moral law. Grant us tension, Lord, in the midst of false peace, and grant us that peace which passes all understanding, in the midst of the struggle in which we are engaged on earth for the dignity of man.

■ Amen.

Holy Communion

■ Jesus, we're here again. What are we doing here?

■ I mean, how is communion with you possible? You're holy, and we're very human. Yet I remember that you also became human.

■ I wonder how we can honestly be nourished and cleansed by your body and blood. Yet I realize communion is an outward and visible sign of an inward and spiritual grace. I accept this mystery.

■ We are grateful for this intimacy with you, Jesus. We thank you for letting us share this corporate action as we offer to God all of creation including our own lives. Give us faith to understand what it means to be thankful.

Prayer for a baptism

■ Don't let this be simply a social occasion, Jesus. Touch the hearts of those present who associate Christianity only with superficiality and have become accustomed to religious exercises devoid of integrity or real meaning.

■ Someone is being baptized into your own life and death, Lord. Someone is being made a member of the church, your own body. Don't let this baptism be shunted off into a small corner of a big church, or into a quiet hour with a handful of people. Let this baptism be a principal part of the whole church's life, Jesus. Make us all realize that we are profoundly involved in it because someone is being ordained to a lifetime of discipleship and ministry in your spirit and name.

Prayer for a confirmation

■ A soldier is seeking active enlistment in your army, Jesus. A pilgrim is asking for a passport which is not of this earth, although it will involve deep and possibly very costly service for you on this earth.

■ Someone wants to share in the sacrament of your body and blood, Lord. Someone seeks to be crucified and risen to new life with you.

■ Thanks for being with us here, Jesus, and sharing your vision of the Kingdom of God with us.

Prayer for a wedding

■ A man and a woman are seeking to become one flesh, Jesus.

■ A man and a woman have decided to throw in their human lot together, and to share and love each other, in sickness and health, in prosperity and poverty, in enthusiasm and despair.

■ A man and a woman want, if they may, to provide the seed and nurture for a family, Lord, and to share in the responsibility of children who will become new men and women.

■ Bless this man and woman, Christ.

An ordination prayer

■ When you say to us "Go," and we comprehend our ministry in the world, do we understand that we will not be contenders in a social popularity contest? Do we perceive that all men and women, including ourselves, prefer to reject your Word rather than accept it? For to accept it means death to the old man and emergence of a new man in fire and love.

■ Do we realize that we are not to go forth into honor or social acceptance, prestige in the community, or increased wealth, even a comfortable status at home or an unchanged interior life?

■ Do we *want* you to call us with your command "Go"? Are we ready for this challenge? Or would we rather you did not call us? Then we could be left alone by you. We would not have to love in the face of hate. We would not have to proclaim your Word to people who will greatly resent it and largely reject it—and us. We could be individual islands in life, untouched by divine commandment and human need. Or could we?

■ Lord, why do you call us when you know our sin, our failures, our inadequacy, our vanity, our absurdity, our weakness? When you call us, will you give us the strength to do what you ask?

A prayer of discipleship

■ "Send me."

■ But where, Lord? To do what?

■ To bring pardon where there had been injury in a life I casually brush against at my daily work? (But I had thought of mediating a teenage gang war in Chicago!)

■ To help turn doubt into faith in a person with whom I live intimately in my circle of family or friends? (But I had thought of helping a tired drunk on skid row!)

■ To bring joy into a life, consumed by sadness, which touches the hem of my life at a drinking fountain? (But I had thought only of a far-off mission land!)

■ "Send me." Send me next door, into the next room, to speak somehow to a human heart beating alongside mine. Send me to bear a note of dignity into a subhuman, hopeless situation. Send me to show forth joy in a moment and a place where there is otherwise no joy but only the will to die.

■ Send me to reflect your light in the darkness of futility, mere existence, and the horror of casual human cruelty. But give me your light, too, Lord, in my own darkness and need.

On work

■ David says he prays without being aware of it when he paints, Jesus. He says this is the real link which keeps him creating and able to function as an artist.

■ Is this true, Lord? Can David's painting be praying? If so, is it possible Richard prays in his Social Work studies, and Henry when he edits his magazine . . . Ruth while she types letters, and Stofer when she cleans people's apartments?

■ Help me to pray that way too, Lord. I want to pray in my doing and being, Jesus.

On dying

■ I heard today about Larry's death, Jesus.

■ My first reaction was sadness because such an honest man and good friend was gone from the scene, Lord. I'll miss him. It seemed to me he always went out of his way to do the best he could about people and things.

■ He made an effort to find out the truth and didn't spare himself in the process. He took an unpopular stand when his beliefs called for it and never seemed to court an easy or sham popularity. He was a loyal friend but also an honest one in offering direct criticism, even when it hurt to give and receive it.

■ I know how lonely his wife will be now and how much she will miss him. Bless his death and resurrection in you, Jesus. Bless his wife's sorrow and stirring of new life.

Here I am in church again, Jesus

■ I love it here, but, as you know, for some of the wrong reasons. I sometimes lose myself completely in the church service and forget the people outside whom you love. I sometimes withdraw far, far inside myself when I am inside church, but people looking at me can see only my pious expression and imagine I am loving you instead of myself.

■ Help us, Lord, who claim to be your special people. Don't let us feel privileged and selfish because you have called us to you. Teach us our responsibilities to you, our brother, and to all the people out there. Save us from the sin of loving religion instead of you.

Prayer of repentance

■ God:

■ Take fire and burn away our guilt and our lying hypocrisies.

■ Take water and wash away our brothers' blood which we have caused to be shed.

■ Take hot sunlight and dry the tears of those we have hurt, and heal their wounded souls, minds, and bodies.

■ Take love and root it in our hearts, so that brotherhood may grow, transforming the dry desert of our prejudices and hatreds.

■ Take our imperfect prayers and purify them, so that we mean what we pray and are prepared to give ourselves to you along with our words, through Jesus Christ, who did not disdain to take our humanness upon him and live among us, sharing our life, our joys, and our pains.

■ Amen.

◼ Afterword

BY WILLIAM ROBERT MILLER

The 1960s have been years of ferment and break-through, certainly of rapid change, in many areas of American life. The decade was barely two months old when sit-ins for racial equality began to sweep through the South, to be followed by the freedom rides and a proliferating movement, primarily among students, that has expanded the goals of freedom across a broad spectrum. A new generation has gone forward from *Lady Chatterley's Lover*, the first uncensored version of which was published in 1959, to a general demand for a new morality based on sexual freedom as a basic right. The America of the sixties is youth-centered, and young people today are finding their own atti-tudes, values, styles of life. They have broken with the past. Their music—rock and roll, folk or electronic —is a breakout from that of previous generations. So is their politics: the new left scorns the dogmas of the old. "Liberal" has come to connote slowness or even hypocrisy in the new vocabulary. From peace demon-strations to discothèque, the pace of life has become fast and forward—à go-go. Already the "new wave" in films has become the standard—Bergman, Polanski, Antonioni represent a new establishment. In art, a fast succession from pop to op and beyond. Camp. Topless. A whole gamut of ways in which the sixties swing, and swing in strikingly new ways.

Within the churches, the 1960s saw the tapering off of the postwar religious boom. Renewal, *aggiornamento,* relevance, secularization and a dozen other catchwords symbolize the new mood. Risk and breakthrough have become operational terms as old patterns of piety in belief and worship crumble and distinctions between Methodist and Baptist, churchman and agnostic, lose their grip. Seminary professors announce that God is dead, and ministers give their lives on the battle line, testifying that Christ is alive. This is not the whole picture, only part of a fleeting glimpse of certain aspects. Something is dying, yet something is coming alive and *happening.* The end of Christendom, a new reformation? One thing is sure: among the same youth who are swinging at the discothèque, there are many who are not only fed up with yesterday's piety but who hunger and thirst for something better—a real and meaningful faith expressed in today's language, *their* language. And not merely Victorian piety cast in hipster talk, not merely official Christianity adapted to the coffee house in order to recruit church members. It is a real hunger and thirst for real meat and drink. For righteousness? Salvation? Never mind the traditional words; the reality is what counts.

A roster of the new voices within the church would include such names as Harvey Cox, author of *The Secular City,* commentator on "the man in the cloverleaf" and *"Playboy's* doctrine of 'male'"; John G. Gensel, Lutheran pastor to the jazz community; Pierre Henri DeLattre, minister and poet among San Francisco's coffee houses; cartoonists Jim Crane and Charles Schultz; apostles of nonviolent direct action Andrew J. Young and Vincent Harding; theologically trained attorneys William Stringfellow and Muriel Gross; inner-city ministers like Howard Moody and James Gusweller. The list barely begins to suggest the emerging new dimensions of ministry involving both clergymen and laymen. Drama at Judson Church, jazz and art exhibits at St. Mark's-in-the-Bouwerie—the thrust is toward meaningful contact and involvement in the world, toward reality. One of the men in the forefront of this thrust is the Rev. Malcolm Boyd, whose life in many ways typifies the new urgency, the new pattern of secularity and renewal on the church's frontiers.

I first heard of Malcolm Boyd as "the espresso priest" in 1961, when he resigned as Episcopal chaplain at Colorado State University. Diocesan officials had decided he was too far out. Soon afterward, when we first began corresponding, he moved to Detroit and subsequently to Washington, D.C. From small, almost ascetic quarters there he has served as the only white member of an interracial team ministry at the Church of the Atonement, in the Negro ghetto of our nation's capital. He was at the same time chaplain-at-large to students on America's college campuses, field secretary of the Episcopal Society for Cultural and Racial Unity, film reviewer for *The Episcopalian*, *The Christian Century* and other church magazines, Washington correspondent for the crusading Protestant monthly, *Renewal*, columnist for the national Negro weekly, *Pittsburgh Courier*, and a few other things.

A press agent's file on Malcolm Boyd would bulge with kudos of all sorts—features in *Time* and *Newsweek* on publication of *Are You Running With Me, Jesus?* or reporting on a performance of his one-act plays before an overflow crowd at Washington Cathedral. A few years ago *Life* included him in a cover story on the "Breakthrough Generation" of America's one hundred men and women under forty most worth watching. In 1962 *Mademoiselle* dubbed him a "disturber of the peace" in a feature-length interview. Out of all this emerges a striking, larger-than-life image—and a trail of questions, like: is he for real?

Who is Malcolm Boyd? He was born on June 8, 1923, in Buffalo, New York, and grew up in New York City. His was a conventional white liberal middle-class childhood. He was brought up as a good Episcopalian and was an acolyte in the parish church. He sang in the choir until his voice changed. He was very studious and got good grades, and he had that kind of naive, churchly faith that he now describes by saying, "I couldn't see out of the stained-glass windows." Later, when he went off to the University of Arizona, he couldn't see into the stained-glass windows. His attitude toward the church was never indifferent—in those days he resented it bitterly for its sham and irrelevance.

After he got his B.A. at the age of twenty, he embarked on a career in Hollywood. For eight years he worked for Mary Pickford, Samuel Goldwyn and a leading advertising agency, Foote, Cone and Belding. He became president of the Television Producers Association of Hollywood and a partner, with Mary Pickford and Buddy Rogers, in PRB Inc., a TV-radio production-packaging firm. It was on the basis of this kind of experience that he was later to score successes with his own plays on racial problems. And it was during this period that he gave the church another try, joining a young adults group and pitching into the parish's activities as an energetic layman with contacts among actors, musicians and other talented Hollywoodians. It was another go at his naive childhood faith, with its illusions about the exalted moral and spiritual stature of the clergy. That comfortable image was rudely shattered when Boyd heard a respected cleric make an anti-Semitic gibe at a Jewish friend who had helped Boyd in his church work. Boyd was so shocked that he simply fled the church, unable to cope with the situation in any other way.

But as he grew more mature, overcoming his illusions about the church, he came to feel that his personal answer lay in engagement rather than escape. In 1951, fed up with the Hollywood rat race, he decided he wanted to become a priest, and he enrolled in the Church Divinity School of the Pacific. When he received his Bachelor of Divinity degree and his holy orders in 1954, he still tended to think of "the church" as the Episcopal Church. But after graduation, he went to Oxford for a year, followed by four months at the Ecumenical Institute of the World Council of Churches at Bossey, Switzerland. Living and studying here, he was brought into intimate daily contact with Christians from many countries and varied traditions. When he left, it was to pursue the ramifications of these contacts in a month-long tour of Europe—not hotel-hopping, but living at a student hostel in Athens, visiting the ancient Greek Orthodox monastery of Mount Athos, staying at a Dominican Center in Paris.

On his return to New York, he studied at Union Theological Seminary. A Negro student was among his classmates. "He was my first 'Negro friend,'" says Malcolm, "and I was his 'white friend.' It says something about our situation in America, doesn't it, if you can reach the age of thirty-two without feeling able to smash such a barrier between persons. It was some years later, in France, that we met again and became just plain *friends*." Malcolm had been reading liberal magazines since early adolescence and had written a vigorous attack on Nazism while in high school, but it was only now that he began to move out beyond principles to real confrontation.

He received the degree of Master of Sacred Theology in 1957. His thesis, the product of eight years in Hollywood and six in the church, was published in book form the same year—*Crisis in Communication*. A probing analysis of our mass media by an informed insider who dares to raise serious moral questions, it is a remarkable document and Malcolm still regards it as the best of his six books except *Are You Running With Me, Jesus?* It was in 1957, too, that Father Boyd went to Taizé, the Protestant monastic community in France. His stay there left a deep impression on him, yet one so complex that even now he has not fully come to a clear understanding of it.

Returning to the United States, Malcolm's first parish was in Indianapolis. It was not long, however, before he was drawn to the campus, and he was given special attention by some—Louisiana State and Mississippi Southern banned him because of his outspoken stand on racial equality. Yet looking back now, Malcolm sees his position then as essentially safe and respectable. Even when he had to leave Colorado State, it was not over a burning issue so much as a matter of style and pace, the swinger versus a starchy hierarchy; and he was still regarded widely as a brilliant young priest, perhaps tomorrow's candidate for a bishopric. He had scarcely moved from Colorado to a new chaplaincy at Wayne State University in Detroit when the newly formed Episcopal Society for Cultural and Racial Unity asked him to join in a freedom ride—a Prayer Pilgrimage for racial equality. He could easily have begged off. Or not so easily. He had to make a hard decision between the accepted liberal verbalizing about race and a more radical commitment which might jeopardize his future in the church. It was a kind of Rubicon. He decided he must go. Later, "civil rights" became fashionable in the church, but it wasn't then, and many who later marched to Washington or at Selma then regarded him as an extremist. It was the first of a dozen such actions. He was later jailed both in the Deep South and in the urban North on charges ranging from violation of a segregation ordinance to disturbing what Boyd calls "the false peace." He took part in a ten and one-half-hour sit-in in Tennessee. He lived in a Freedom House that had been bombed in McComb, Mississippi. He picketed the Episcopal Cathedral in Atlanta to protest its holding commencement exercises of a school that excluded Negroes. Back in Michigan, too, he followed through. On one occasion in Dearborn, he says, the atmosphere was more charged with fear than anywhere he had seen in the South. In Detroit, Father Boyd was the only priest for three hours on a picket line protesting employment policies at General Motors. In 1964 he logged 1,100 miles of travel in rural Mississippi in company with a Roman Catholic journalist, William Jacobs. It was a journey full of tension and danger—the same danger that took the lives of three young men that summer. Out of their interviews with both the poor and dispossessed and the Establishment spokesmen, they wrote a series of articles for *Ave Maria* which subsequently won them the Catholic Press Association's award for the best Civil Rights reporting of the year.

The 1961 Prayer Pilgrimage experience spurred Malcolm to write his first play, "Boy." He makes no claims for himself as a dramatist, describing his plays as "a frank attempt to disturb audiences and puncture smugness about human injustice." I would say the attempt is successful, to put it mildly. I first met Malcolm after a performance of three of the plays at Union Theological Seminary in 1963—"Boy," "Study in Color" and "The Job." The theater was packed to standing room, and we had barely enough time afterward for a minute's conversation before the audience, well disturbed, filled the social hall to discuss the plays' implications. Malcolm has acted in his own plays—convincingly, I can testify—on campuses from coast to coast. In 1964, "Boy" was slated for broadcast on WMSB-TV at Michigan State University, but it was sidetracked on grounds that it contained "obscene and vulgar language." The offending words were "damn" and "nigger." Subsequently the banned sequence was broadcast from coast to coast by NBC-TV. Meanwhile, the American Civil Liberties Union championed Boyd's right to be heard, and the Anti-Defamation League of B'nai B'rith distributed the plays nationally on film. Boyd's bishop, who had not seen a production of the play, attacked Malcolm in a church publication for bowing to what he termed the avant-garde use of "obscenity and vulgarity" in the play. When the wire services picked up the story, the incident became an international *cause célèbre*. Father Boyd had been asked to resign several months earlier for his three years of Establishment boat-rocking and radical commitment. Now he complied with the request, moving from Detroit to his new, nationally scaled duties based in Washington.

It was in 1963 that Malcolm and I began working together. I had been impressed by the caliber of his film reviews in *The Episcopalian,* and as managing editor of *United Church Herald* at that time, I saw no reason why the same column could not be made available to a whole new group of readers. The kickoff was a feature article on what makes a good religious film, and it was soon followed regularly by a monthly page, "Malcolm Boyd On Film," which has subsequently appeared in *Presbyterian Survey, The Canadian Churchman* and other magazines.

When I left the *Herald* to become a book editor at Holt, Rinehart and Winston, we kept in touch, and it was natural that before long Malcolm sent me a book manuscript. Actually it was not quite a book manuscript, but rather an assortment of some thirty-odd prayers, beginning with one titled "Are You Running With Me, Jesus?" They were all very much Malcolm Boyd in their range of concerns, their honesty and directness, and they were, so to speak, like stenographic transcripts of situations in which he had prayed in just this way, with just these words. Knowing Malcolm as I did, they rang true. The idea of such a book was very unorthodox, if not unique. I showed the prayers to William Stringfellow, who liked them very much, and to a number of others. I was astonished at the way the readers were polarized by them—they either responded eagerly or were offended by their directness and lack of ecclesiastical finesse. It was not a safe book; it was a risk. But it was not merely because Malcolm was my friend that I decided to go ahead with it—I felt strongly that there was a need for such a book.

But we still didn't have a *book*. In fact, we were a long way from it, as I explained to the author. There would have to be three times as many prayers, and they should not be concocted to fill a prescription. I made a few suggestions. "Malcolm, you've known jazz musicians and you've known assembly-line workers. They belong in the book, too." And after some reflection, Malcolm would remember a particular occasion, an individual, and how he had prayed, and he would write it down.

Some of my fellow editors suggested that we drop the "Meditations On Films." I knew these meditations had special significance for Malcolm, but I asked him how he felt. He did not insist, but they meant a lot to him. He wanted them in. They stayed in. Some eyebrows were raised over "Prayers For Sexual Freedom," but we closed ranks and went ahead. We struggled over certain prayers, not many, which would not make sense unless they said more about the situation with which they dealt. Most often, Malcolm dug deeper into his recollections until the picture emerged in focus. In some instances a prayer remained obscure, too dependent on private meaning or requiring far too lengthy an explanation of the situation. Perhaps a dozen of these were dropped. But finally, after many meetings, 'phone calls and letters, we had a book. And what a book! *Publishers' Weekly* called it, six months after publication, "the surprise religious best seller of the year," and a Protestant church leader, speaking at a denominational board meeting, termed it "the most influential prayerbook of this generation."

In an article in *The Churchman*, Malcolm wrote: "The church's mission is to engage in dialogue . . . [It] involves the exposure of papier-mâché publicity images of itself or any other part of the society, because valid images reflect only realities . . . A church is dead if it cannot communicate the gospel of love for which it exists." In large part this statement is not only a description of the mission of the church; it is also Malcolm Boyd's personal credo, one reason why he has been called "The Communicator." He has communicated in many ways, engaging in private dialogue with a troubled student, writing and performing in plays, acting out his witness for social justice in demonstrations, writing about films, addressing large gatherings. Soon after he moved from Detroit to Washington, he appeared at a night club, the Show Boat—not a stand-up comic but a stand-up priest, communicating in thought-provoking words like those in this book, images of reality, backed up by Charlie Byrd and his trio. Later, guitarist Charlie Byrd and Malcolm Boyd appeared together in Washington's National Cathedral, offering prayers from *Are You Running With*

Me, Jesus? to a record crowd of six thousand people who jammed every available inch of that stately gothic structure. On Good Friday, 1966, at the invitation of the Protestant Council of the City of New York, the priest and the guitarist did a three-hour reading of the prayers at historic Broadway United Church of Christ. It was one of the most authentic worship experiences I have ever witnessed. Shortly before this, Malcolm had been at a Negro church on Chicago's South Side, reading his prayers in alternation with jazz by Oscar Brown Jr. And not long after, at the auditorium of Catholic University in Washington, he read selections to a thousand nuns, priests, and seminarians. Incidentally, when the Rt. Rev. Paul Moore Jr., suffragan bishop of the diocese of Washington, visited Pope Paul VI at the Vatican, he presented him with a copy of the book inscribed "To Your Holiness. Love, Malcolm." Whether in a cathedral or a place like Arthur's Discothèque or the Show Boat, or on radio or TV, he communicates this unadorned earnestness.

I have known few people with the drive, stamina, and sheer restlessness of Malcolm Boyd. The title of this book is right for him, because he is always on the run. The first thing you notice about him in conversation is his eyes. He looks you square in the face, and those eyes tell you he is absolutely on the level, completely honest, and serious. They are the eyes of a man who has quite obviously a keen mind, who has not only knowledge and insight but certain unshakable convictions—and at the same time an element of questioning, a trace of personal self-doubt.

In April 1965, Malcolm was the keynote speaker at the annual meeting of the Associated Church Press in Ottawa. In his hotel room the night before, he read his speech to me paragraph by paragraph, asking me to slash away at it with any criticism that occurred to me. Almost without fail, he amended his text whenever I suggested that he could make this or that point clearer. He did this because he felt that I knew the audience better than he—church magazine editors representing the gamut of American Protestantism from large to small denominations and from liberal to conservative. What did I think of his speech on the whole, on the basis of past ACP Conventions I had attended? It was pretty strong—a head-on challenge to overcome irrelevance in the church, and a virtual indictment of many church magazines. "You can count on a pretty shrill reaction from some of them," I said. Malcolm gave me that troubled, on-the-spot look of his and then smiled. "Well, it's true, isn't it?"

The next morning I heard him give the speech, and he was, if anything, even harder-hitting than I expected, having added two or three barbed remarks. Not one church editor rose to dispute him afterward. Some of them swallowed hard, but they listened. Discussion was lively, but it was on Malcolm's terms. His speech sounded a keynote that reverberated for the rest of the three-day convention.

A few weeks later we were together at a small but prestigious college in upstate New York. He had gone there, as he often does, with no honorarium in sight, just round-trip travel expenses; and the conservative "chapel rats" had done a very feeble job of publicizing the meeting. The gathering was small, but Malcolm took it in stride. As always, he minced no words. The majority he sized up as a lot of rich kids putting on a beatnik pose. He told them so, and went on to ask them what it meant, really, deep down—and where would they go from here, what would they do with their lives out in the real world after fun-and-games were over? He was not merely putting them down or telling them off—he was "telling it like it is." Instead of playing along with their notions of nonconformity, he left them something to think about. And he responded freely and candidly to questions of all kinds—about the freedom movement, about sex, the war in Viet Nam, the church—not as a pundit but as a man of experience who knows the score and knows how to make up his mind.

By the time the meeting was over, a handful of students remained. They were the committed ones, the ones who already had some real sense of direction, such as the boy who was active in a local campaign to eliminate racial discrimination in housing and employment. A casual onlooker would readily have believed that Malcolm was a frequent visitor to this campus (it was his first time) and was catching up on the latest doings of close friends. They were in fact friends of an hour or two—and yes, they were among his closest friends. Afterward, on the long car ride to New York City, their problems and statements were still specific and real to him. To Malcolm Boyd, involvement is more than a catchword; it is a way of life. He dislikes the form of the sermon; for him, preaching the gospel is the response that occurs in unpremeditated encounters like this, on a put-up-or-shut-up basis.

For a month in the fall of 1966 Malcolm became involved in an experience which quickly assumed international significance. He opened an engagement at San Francisco's cellar nightclub, the hungry i. On the same bill was comedian Dick Gregory, with whom he had been jailed in Chicago earlier in the year following a civil rights demonstration. Malcolm read prayers from *Are You Running With Me, Jesus?*, interspersing these with running comments on such themes as peace, race, sex, cinema, and updated religion. Peter Yarrow of Peter, Paul, and Mary accompanied him on the guitar as Malcolm also read several "secular meditations" from his book *Free To Live, Free To Die*. Afterwards Malcolm invited the patrons in the hungry i to ask him any questions they had. This kind of free-flowing dialogue with the audience was Malcolm's favorite part of the whole hungry i experience, he told me when I phoned him on opening night. He also said how pleased he was that he could contribute the $1000 a week he was being paid to the freedom movement.

Malcolm was a good draw at the hungry i. His stint there led to offers from other night spots in New York, Washington, Las Vegas, Chicago, and London. He likes the challenge of the spotlight—and the very non-churchly atmosphere. Some people come out of curiosity, some because they have read the book or heard the recording, others to heckle him. Malcolm gets through to them. "And they get through to me," he says. "It's a mutual involvement we have with one another." Among the many letters and postcards he received (around fifty a day) during his gig at the hungry i, this one stands out: "I want to apologize for giving you a hard time Wednesday night. I had too much to drink." Both the heckling and the apology showed honesty. "This is why I like the night club

■ 153

bit," says Malcolm. "In a parish church you seldom can guess what's behind the pious masks people wear. Here the masks are off."

Press comments about Malcolm's hungry i appearance came from European television to U. S. *Life*, from newspapers in New Delhi, Buenos Aires, Rome and Addis Ababa to NBC-TV's Huntley-Brinkley news program. Malcolm said the entire episode reminded him of the play *Rashomon*, which concerns fascinatingly different points of view about a single event. *The New York Times Mazgazine* commented that "Father Boyd is a spectacular example of the church's new thrust into secular life" and went on to describe him as "a latter-day Luther or a more worldly Wesley trying to move organized religion out of 'ghettoized' churches into the streets, the business offices, the union halls, the CORE chapters, the theaters, and even the night clubs where the people are."

No account of Malcolm Boyd would be complete without acknowledging that he rubs some people the wrong way. There are those who don't want him to disturb their peace, who want to keep not only Malcolm Boyd but Jesus Christ at a safe distance from their lives. And there are those, too, who do not disagree with what Malcolm stands for but regard him as a colossal egotist and publicity hound. The good press agent's answer to this would be that it just isn't so. Malcolm himself is all too ready to reply with an abashed *"Mea culpa."* He knows his own weaknesses and is not defensive about them. If he rates high in egotism, he rates zero in hypocrisy, and there is genuine humility in his self-awareness. Being a priest doesn't mean that he isn't human or that he has attained instant sainthood—a fact he learned in Hollywood years ago. And a man with so much drive, with so much to say, is not inclined to be shy of the spotlight. Paradoxically, Malcolm lacks the guile to dampen his exuberance, to keep cool when he seeks attention. Far from having a Messianic complex, he is more receptive to criticism and advice than anyone else I know.

Malcolm Boyd is the kind of consecrated egotist who believes that everything depends on him. Like many men of this temperament, he finds it hard to say no when demands are made upon him. He wants to be heard, to be effective. But it is more than that. He will literally lose sleep in order to listen attentively to a student in need of advice on an urgent personal problem or, as often as not, simply functioning as confessor. Many students write to him, not seeking a reply at all, but just because it helps them to cope with their problems, knowing they are shared with someone who cares. Malcolm also forfeits sleep in order to keep up with what's happening in modern fiction, theater, films—all sources of understanding the human situation, hence vital to his priesthood. He drives himself to the limit. It has become a cliché; instead of "goodbye," I tell him "get some rest." And he promises to do so—sometimes. In 1965, the projected vacation period was transformed into several weeks of touring the Freedom Schools in Mississippi and Alabama with four young Negro veterans of the freedom movement. Sleeping on the plank floors of shacks, often getting only one meal a day, subjected to police harassment and more than one attempt on their lives, it was far from restful. I remember when he took on this assignment. He had no illusions about what it would be like. He needed rest. But he had to do it—and it was without personal fanfare, without income. Immediately afterward, he was in the Watts section of Los Angeles, within a few hours after the outbreak of the devastating riots. It only remains to add the front-page news that greeted him as he settled into his seat on the plane when he left Los Angeles: the slaying of Jonathan Daniels, young Episcopal seminarian who had been with him in Selma, one of the stops on Boyd's tour. I have seen Malcolm Boyd in rare moments of relaxation among friends, with no schedule to meet—really relaxed, with his feet up for a whole day. Even then, I could see plainly that as soon as the spring was uncoiled, it began winding up again for the next long sprint of "running with Jesus." Incidentally, the visit to Watts resulted in Malcolm's *Christian Century* article, "Violence in Los Angeles," one of the best examples of news reporting I have seen anywhere; and from the weeks of hardship in the Deep South came a probing, in-depth article for *Christianity and Crisis*, "Maintaining Humanness in the Freedom Movement."

Who is Malcolm Boyd? He is a man on the run who knows he can't make it alone. There is egotistical candor, which is a true form of humility, in the way he puts the question. He knows he is running, but "are you running with me, Jesus?" It is not mere rhetoric, for there is in this question the confession of a man brimming with intelligent concern for others, of a man with a deep sense of what is real and meaningful in life—a confession that ultimately, in every moment, his sense of direction and equilibrium must come from a source higher than self, deeper than ego.

Who is Malcolm Boyd? Some see him only in a church pulpit or as a priest at a parish altar. Others see him only as a figure on a picket line, or within the inner city, or on a lecture platform, or in a coffee house. Among those who know him in greater depth are the students with whom he meets, at universities across the nation, during the night hours *after* the formal meetings are over. Countless times, in conversation, he has referred to these encounters. Some of the best prayers in this book arose in those night hours. The students are black and white, men and women. Malcolm talks with them in apartments near the campus, in the back rooms of beer joints, in dormitory rooms, in the desolate interiors of coffee houses, *after* midnight and sometimes all night. "I shed my blood and they shed theirs," he says—a real confrontation occurs; no subjects are taboo, no one stands on propriety or status. In this kind of sharing, Malcolm Boyd gives himself to the student generation. What does he get in return? In his own words: "What it takes to go on living."

Who is Malcolm Boyd? He is a man of God—not because he wears a clerical collar and can use theological lingo, but because his life reflects, with all the secular and vernacular accents of today, what it means to be a follower of Jesus Christ. That is what the prayer of the book's title is about. It is not the prayer of someone who has reduced faith to an abstract formula. Real faith is not like that. It has in it the pulse of life, not metronomic but swinging with a blues beat that leaves room for riffs and improvisation.

■ 157

That is why a man of God has to pray, and why Malcolm Boyd prays as he does. Every one of these prayers is a prayer for freedom, a prayer of freedom. Notice how often the prayers tell rather than ask—the crux of them all is "Lead, Lord." There is no paradox here. A modern man of God has no time for silly self-abasement, but he knows he needs guidance beyond himself in order to *be* himself—and God knows this too. The Jesus to whom Boyd prays is the same one found in the New Testament—not sitting back in celestial splendor craving praise and wordy adulation, but ready to respond with love to human need, ready to run with those who seek him out. The prayers in this book testify better than any biography: this is Malcolm Boyd, a man like you and me, freely speaking from the depths of his soul to find support and guidance in every kind of situation that life presents—as we all must do, each in his own way. Who is Malcolm Boyd? I have told a good deal of the answer that I know. But as a man of God, Malcolm would turn the question around, asking, along with Jesus: Who are you? It is a good question for each of us to confront, and this book will help us to find answers.

It
speaks
for
itself.

STEREO
CS 9519
CL 9519
COLUMBIA

◄═══ STEREO ═══►
360 SOUND

**Are You Running
With Me, Jesus?**
Prayers by
Malcolm Boyd
Guitar Accompaniment
Charlie Byrd

On COLUMBIA RECORDS